To Tom

from John', Mel

Ay 4, 2022

MW01295173

Acknowledgments

I would like to thank my husband, Captain John Wood, who made our dream of living in the Caribbean a reality. I thank my mother, the late Pat Guthrie, who I will always think of as my biggest fan. I thank John's parents, Bill Wood and the late Ann Wood, for installing a love of travel in their son and for their unending support of our lifestyle.

I want to thank Lori Soule for the encouragement she provided and for the many hours she spent proofreading, especially in the beginning of the process. Without Lori's unending support, I would have given up long ago.

When it came time to order a printed proof of the book, there was no way to ship a copy to Roatan. The COVID-19 crisis resulted in the closure of our borders and our airport. I needed to find a few volunteers to be my eyes!

My Aunt Jeanette and Uncle Jack Stubbs agreed to have a copy shipped to their address in Canada. Jan, as she is known to most people, has been a continued source of support during our years of travel and I thank her and Jack for their input.

Cindy Darby also agreed to let me ship a copy to her address in Las Vegas, NV. Even better, she offered her sister, Bobbi Martin's help. Bobbi is employed by the Clark County School District as a learning strategist to support teachers that have difficulties. Cindy read the digital proof, while Bobbi edited the printed proof.

It takes a team to write a book!

"There are no foreign lands. It is the traveler only who is foreign."
— Robert Louis Stevenson

Cover and book design by Melanie Wood
Editing by Bobbi Martin
Illustrations by Melanie Wood
Photos by Melanie and John Wood
Printed in the United States

Published by Diamond Lil Publications
Port Royal, Roatan, Honduras
504-3365-1105
johnmelw@hotmail.com

Mexico

Belize

Gulf of Honduras

Utila   Roatan   Guanaja

Caribbean Sea

Guatemala

Honduras

El Salvador

Nicaragua

Costa Rica

Pacific Ocean

Panama

Diamond Lil Does Roatan

Chapter 1

Dec 7, 2008

The only comforting thought when you lose an engine, while out at sea, is knowing that we have two of them! Neither Captain John nor I were looking forward to the long trip to Roatan on just one engine. Therefore, when a weather window presented itself, even though we hadn't had much chance to explore the Sapodilla Islands of Belize, we agreed that it was time to head out. Wind from the west, which was rare, would be perfect for our trip on just one engine.

After six long months of life in the steamy rainforest of the Rio Dulce, I longed for the turquoise water and sandy beaches of the Caribbean Sea. I had enjoyed our second season in the Rio Dulce. However, it was the Honduran Bay Islands I longed for. Finally, we were on our way.

"Let's stop in the Sapodilla Cays for a couple of days, honey," I suggested, as we planned our departure from the Rio. The islands are popular among Guatemalans, Hondurans, and Belizeans for vacationing. It seemed that every cruiser we talked to had been there, except us.

The captain agreed, and we planned the short, 30-mile trip from Livingston to the Sapodilla Islands. I was giddy with excitement at the prospect of a short ocean cruise and a night or two in Caribbean heaven.

However, like Captain Ron, from the movie by the same name, says, "If it's going to happen, it's going to happen out there." Our initial sense of exhilaration, as we set off across the open sea, was short-lived, as the port side transmission failed.

John had repaired it when we reached the Rio last June. It had worked like a charm on three separate shakedown cruises along the Rio Dulce from Bruno's Marina to Texan Bay and back, over the summer.

"I can't do anything until we get to Roatan," John told me. "We'll have to make the crossing on one engine."

A dismal, cloudy sky and a choppy, grey sea didn't live up to the turquoise splendor I had anticipated as we lurched and rolled our way to the Sapodillas.

We were granted a temporary visitor's pass by the Belizean immigration officials on Hunting Cay and were welcomed back to life at sea as we rocked and rolled our way through a sleepless night.

Dec 8, 2008

Our chart plotter indicated a time of 21 1/2 hours to reach West End, Roatan, our destination. If we left Hunting Cay by 11:30 am, we would arrive in West End around 8:00 am the following morning. We set off with a light west wind and a flat calm, following sea, our favorite. I scanned the horizon for the telltale peaks that mean large waves and was relieved to see nothing terribly daunting.

The wind changed, however, as we made our way east. It clocked around to the north, creating a beam sea, hitting us broadside, our least favorite sea condition. The speed that our original calculation was based upon left us lurching and rolling with boat contents crashing and falling all over the place, so we sped the one engine up a little, making life on board slightly less miserable.

The sea laid down nicely by about 10:00 pm and the clouds parted, presenting us with a partial moon. The sea sparkled below, and the stars in the sky glittered above. We took turns napping, for three hours each. During my watch, I didn't see a single light on the radar, not a vessel out there except us.

Past the island of Utila I went, and on towards West End, while the captain slept peacefully in our cabin below. I wanted to let him sleep longer and surprise him when we arrived, but we were getting close too soon.

I knew that we needed to slow down so we would have daylight to enter the cut. However, a change in engine speed would wake him instantly. That was our signal that I needed some help on the helm, but I had no choice.

By 6:45 am, we were secured to a mooring ball in the mooring field between West End and West Bay. We tidied up the boat, made a log entry, went to bed, and slept until noon. When we woke up, surrounded by crystal-clear, aquamarine water, the agonies of the previous night were quickly forgotten.

We both agreed that absence does indeed make the

heart grow fonder. The six months away made us see the beauty of Roatan through new eyes. We agreed that the two tropical paradises, the Rio Dulce and the Honduras Bay Islands, couldn't be more diverse in their beauty. There are countless shades of green in the jungle and out here, an equal number of shades of blue.

Dec 15, 2008

We arrived in West End nine days ago. I have no idea where the time has gone!

When we packed into the crowded little van that passes for a bus and traveled into Coxen Hole, last week, to check into Honduras, we discovered a new government statute in effect. Our passports now need to be stamped at the airport, and not at the Port Captain's office, like last year. Retracing our steps, we hiked a couple of miles to the airport and a couple of miles back to Coxen Hole, stopping along the way for some Bojangles chicken, Honduras' version of our own Kentucky Fried Chicken.

After our artery-clogging feast, we continued into downtown Coxen Hole. John went to the customs office while I headed for the post office to mail some gifts to the kids in Canada. We were back on island time. We waited patiently for the post office to open after their usual lunch break. When they finally re-opened, around 2:00 pm, the friendly clerk said, "I'm sorry, but you'll have to come back. The girl with the stamps isn't here right now. She should be back at around 4 o'clock."

Hot, tired, and exasperated, Captain John hoofed it down towards the cruise ship docks to the hardware store, while I sat and enjoyed a cold *cervesa* and enjoyed a little people watching.

We picked up a new cell phone and a few items that we hadn't been able to buy in the Rio Dulce; paper plates, rye whiskey, muffin tins, Alfredo sauce, and baking soda. Decadent!

Mother Nature has now held us captive on *Diamond Lil* for two days, as the wind howls from the west. As nasty as this is, we cannot leave the boat unattended in such windy weather. The canvas over the aft deck had to be folded back and tied down with bungee cords to prevent the wind from tearing it. We spent two days napping, reading, and staring out to sea.

Finally, the wind clocked around, and we were back to the prevailing east winds that make the anchorage at West End so popular.

John is planning to call someone in Alaska who has a used transmission for sale. It couldn't be much further away, and it will be interesting to see what the shipping quote is. Until then, we are not going anywhere fast. Then again, who would want to?

December 24, 2008

Where does time go? I am amazed that we are spending our fourth Christmas in the Caribbean. John dropped me off on the shore by the Barefoot Beach Bar this morning, where the route for the public bus from West End to Coxen Hole begins. By the time we followed the dusty little road that leads into *La Colonia*, a small *barrio* (town), along the way, the van was packed with passengers. There is always room for one more, it seems. I sat squished up tight against a friendly girl named Vanessa. She was on her way to work at Carambola Gardens, she told me.

Carambola Botanical Gardens is a popular destination just a few miles outside of West End and one of the tours of choice for the flocks of cruise ship visitors to the island. I was full of questions about the flora along the bus route. I'm trying to learn to identify all the plants and trees on the island, a daunting task because there are countless species.

Shopping is a challenge. The only Christmas gifts that John asked for were a sturdy, rechargeable flashlight for the boat and some new boxer shorts. I did the Coxen Hole crawl, from *tienda* to *tienda,* using my best Spanish, asking for *"un foco muy grande y recargable?"*

The clerks shouted down the street to their fellow shop keepers to see if anyone else had the item I was searching for. After two hours of traipsing up and down hot, dusty streets, I found not one single rechargeable flashlight. After a third hour, I found the only two pairs of boxer shorts that even slightly resemble the kind that John likes to wear.

Over and over, shopkeepers held up tiny little pairs of clingy briefs. *"Mas grande, mas grande, y mas flojo."* Much bigger, much bigger, and looser,"I repeated. *"Para mi esposo."* For my husband. I came away wondering just what all the Honduran men on the street were wearing under their pants.

Signs advertising turkey dinners are slowly popping up around town. It seems we have several to choose from, which is fine by me. Cooking a turkey dinner in the boat, besides the fact that there is no turkey for sale in this town, is not fun, especially when it comes to washing dishes!

We will wander up and down the sandy little seaside road in West End, park ourselves somewhere on the sand, and enjoy our turkey dinner with a million-dollar view.

People are wishing each other Merry Christmas, *or Feliz Navidad,* as they pass each other in the shops and on the street. Tonight, there is live music at the Barefoot Beach Bar at our end of the strip. I'll see if I can keep the captain awake long enough to take me there.

He bought me the very last carton of *ron popo,* or eggnog, in the grocery store in Coxen Hole yesterday so I had a couple of rum and egg nogs last night. I thought of all my family and friends and how I miss smelling the wood smoke and admiring the way the lights color the

snow. Yes, I miss the snow, well for a few, rum-
enhanced moments at least.

Feliz Navidad

January 1, 2009

Feliz Neuvo Ano!

We brought in the New Year with friends Cheryl and
Mike, from S/V *Let It Be*. (The acronym S/V refers to a
sailing vessel. M/V would refer to a motor vessel) We
first met at them at Texan Bay Marina in the Rio Dulce
this past summer and became good friends. They are
from Boston, Massachusetts. We get a kick out of their
heavy New England drawl.

At first, they struck us as an odd couple. Mike was an
energetic extrovert with a booming voice. His dark
brown eyes sparkled mischievously. He wore his long,
greying hair back in a ponytail under a variety of sporty
caps and sported an equally long mustache. At times he
refers to himself as Miguel, the Spanish version of Mike.

Cheryl was much quieter, with bright blue eyes that
glimmered from her rounded, tanned face. She wore her
sandy brown hair parted in the middle and tied back.

We enjoyed a New Year's dinner and a few drinks
aboard *Let It Be*, before taking the dinghy to shore for
some dancing at Foster's Nightclub. Unlike last year,
when we were anchored in Jonesville and were in bed by
8:00 pm, this year we managed to stay awake until
midnight!

John, on the bow of *Diamond Lil*, as we head out to sea

Sharing the sea with big ships

John, checking the port side transmission

Early morning arrival in West End, Roatan

The Honduran Bay Islands

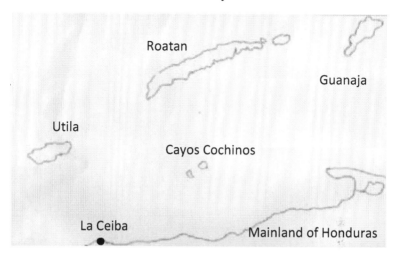

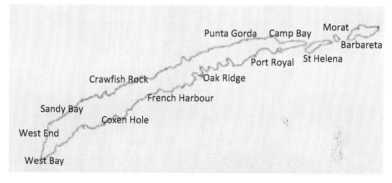

The Island of Roatan and one of my paintings

Chapter 2

January 7, 2009

As we sipped our coffee this morning, anticipating another perfect day in the idyllic anchorage of West End, we were startled by a loud BANG! A deafening silence followed the bang. Our generator, which we nicknamed *"the beast,"* had stopped running. John swore, slid off his seat in the cabin, stepped down the one step to the aft deck, and lifted the cover of the starboard side hatch.

"THAT'S IT! I GIVE UP!" he declared, as he pointed to a large black hole in the generator. He reached down and picked up a greasy piece of thick, red metal about the size of a golf ball.

"We blew a hole right through the side of the fucking block," he cursed.

Things were breaking faster than we could fix them. Right then and there, the idea hit me. I needed a job.

John rolled his eyes when I suggested the plan. That didn't deter me. The town is full of ex-pats, working in stores, bars, and restaurants. Surely, I could find a job, I thought. If I did, I would be more likely to convince John to stay here. He doesn't love West End as much as I do. It is more expensive to live here than other places on the island, he complains.

I hit the pavement, figuratively, that is. I wandered along the white, sandy road through town. My first stop was at Eagle Ray's Restaurant. The manager told me that they didn't hire gringos.

"The Lighthouse Restaurant does, though," he said, "and they are looking for someone." Casey, a girl I met at the internet café recently, works there, and she told me the same thing when we spoke.

I found Johnna Ebanks, owner/manager of the Lighthouse Restaurant, working in her store in front of the restaurant, selling souvenirs.

She was a white woman of average height, and larger than average width, with blond hair, and a pale complexion.

"Hi, my name is Melanie," I said. John and I had eaten at her place a few times, so she recognized me. "Are you doing any hiring?" I asked.

"What type of hiring?" she asked me.

"Serving," I replied.

"Have you served tables before?" she questioned.

"Yes," I assured her.

"What is your availability?" she asked.

I explained that I was totally open - days, nights, or weekends - whatever she required.

"Stop back after 4:00 pm, when both girls who would like to give up a few shifts are working, and we'll see what we can work out," she replied.

The money was not great, she told me. I would make 200 lempiras ($10.00 US) a night for working from 4:00 pm until the last customer paid, with the kitchen closing at 10:00 p.m. Tips would be shared between kitchen, bar, and serving staff. Both tips and wages would be paid daily.

I returned at 4:00 pm. Johnna asked whether I was in the mood to work or would prefer to start tomorrow. John had made plans to get together with friends Mike and Cheryl, before Cheryl flew back to the States for two weeks, or I would have started then and there. I returned at 4:00 pm the next day and began to work. There was no application form to fill out. I wasn't even asked my last name. I had a job.

Johnna spent most of the evening sitting quietly on a bar stool beside the cash register. She greeted the guests, oversaw everything that went on in the restaurant, prepared all the bills, handled all the cash, and bid the guests goodnight. She practically blended into the scenery after a while, so inconspicuous was her manner.

She was married to Sam, the head chef. They were as opposite in nature as in physical appearance. Sam was an energetic black man with a distinct, booming voice, who could be heard coming before he was seen. His disposition was as extroverted as hers was introverted. He was known for his quick temper. Each time he pushed open the swinging door to the kitchen and strode in, I could feel the tension in the room rise a few degrees.

"The most important thing to remember," Johnna told me that first night, "is that my husband can be an asshole. Don't let him get to you. His bark is worse than his bite. If you have any problems, just talk to me."

I had worked for temperamental chefs in the past. I was good at avoiding conflicts and didn't let the warning dampen my new working girl spirits.

I considered the first night I spent waiting tables in paradise a success since I didn't spill, break, or drop anything or serve anyone the wrong meal.

It was a quiet night and my portion of the tips came to 180 lempiras or just under $10.00. After seven hours of work, I came away with just under $20.00 Was it worth it? Did I go back?

Yes, I did. Saturday night was my second shift, and it was another quiet night. My total earnings were 530 lempiras or $26.50. Under the Canadian system, I would have walked away with much more, as my tips were generous. Here, the tips had to be split many ways. There were three servers, two cooks, a bartender, two dishwashers, and a salad/bread person. That made nine people with their hands in the pie!

On night number three, my total earnings were $27.10. On my first day shift, from 7:00 am till 4:00 pm, my total wages were $10.00, my share of the tips $5.00, making $15.00 for 9 hours of work. I am getting a good feel for the pittance that locals manage to live on. Even my meager wage is more than most of them earn.

"No! Don't do that!" said one of my co-workers on my

first night of work. I was scraping the uneaten food from a customer's plate into the garbage.

"Put it here," said the girl, as she lifted the tablecloth which hung down from a counter, covering a set of shelves below. She popped open the lid to her plastic storage container and pointed inside.

"You can put it in mine too," said the other girl working that night. "I take it home to feed to my kids."

I did as I was told, feeling somewhat shocked that these women would take uneaten food, from a stranger's plate, home to their families. Nothing much except fish bones and lobster shells gets as far as the garbage. It is scooped off plates as they come into the kitchen and either eaten or packed away to take home.

On my third night of work, two girls that I knew came in for dinner. They ordered the three-cheese crab dip for an appetizer. As was often the case, their meal arrived just moments after the appetizer. They set the large plate of crab dip aside and dug into their equally huge seafood platters.

When they were finished, I scooped up the barely touched crab dip and took it home to the captain. From that time on, we dined on lobster tails, crab legs, and decadent dishes from both land and sea. Sam, although he was a crusty bugger, was a good chef. His claim to fame was cooking for former President, Bill Clinton. The money wasn't great, but the fringe benefits were.

January 14, 2009

This morning, I dragged the captain, who has been under the weather for the past few days, to the clinic at Anthony's Key Resort. We hopped into a *collectivo*, which is a regular taxi, but one that you share with other passengers. They are much less expensive than private taxis, and since there is basically only one road on the island, stopping to pick up or drop off the other passengers only takes a few seconds.

Anthony's Key is one of the original resorts on the island, boasting more than 40 years in business. It offers an excellent medical clinic as well as the only hyperbaric chamber on the island, a lifesaver for any diver who suffers from the bends.

High on the list of popular tourist attractions on the island is the Dive with the Dolphins Encounter at Anthony's Key Resort. Together with the Roatan Institute for Marine Sciences, AKR offers a wide variety of dolphin programs.

The popular Dolphin Encounter, held in waist-high, crystal clear water, does not require swimming. A brief information session is followed by a 25-minute, up-close, and personal petting session with one of the friendly mammals. Photos may be taken with personal cameras or purchased by professional photographers on site.

The Dolphin Snorkel, in addition to the information session and the initial 25 minutes with one dolphin, offers an additional 30 minutes of snorkeling time with a dozen or more dolphins. This program costs a little more than the encounter.

The Dolphin Dive, which requires visitors to present a certification card to participate, begins with the topside instructions and a question and answer period. Guests enjoy a 5-minute boat ride to the reef wall and are lowered to a sandy bottom, 60 feet below the surface where they may interact with dolphins in a natural setting for 45 minutes.

AKR also offers a six-day camp for children, a great option for families where the parents wish to participate in off-site dives knowing that their children are enjoying a safe and educational experience.

For students and avid dolphin lovers, there is also a "Trainer for a Day" and a "Two-day Dolphin Specialty" course offered.

We enjoyed the air conditioning inside the medical clinic, as we sat with our number in hand, waiting for our turn to see the doctor. The huge hyperbaric chamber takes up about a third of the waiting area.

The diagnosis was a urinary tract infection. The total cost of the doctor's visit, a two-week course of antibiotics, and pain medication was 400 lempiras, or $20.00 US.

We were told that most gringos living in Central America develop parasites in their digestive system. I was tested, and the results were negative! We are relieved to be in the minority in this case. The doctor said that if one of us had them we both would, so we can assume that we are both parasite-free.

The mooring field here in West End emptied out a couple of days ago as a cold front approached. There were 20 boats here before that. Now, there are only two left, *Diamond Lil* and a sailboat whose crew members are waiting for an engine part to arrive before they can move. Luckily, the front hasn't amounted to much, at least not yet. We have had plenty of rain but not much wind.

We opened the top of our water tank and let Mother Nature fill it. One day, Miguel and Cheryl, our sailing friends from Boston, watched us fill our water tanks from jerry cans we had hauled from shore in our dinghy. They asked us why we didn't just leave the screw-on lid to our water tank off and let it fill with rainwater. They showed us how they positioned a cloth just below the opening to the tank on our side deck to dam up the water and fill the tank. We looked at each other, thinking the same thing. After four years of cruising, why didn't we think of that?

I sold another web-exclusive article to *PassageMaker Magazine*, for mid-February publishing. The title of this one is "A Rio Retirement Alternative". I figured out that I would have to work 17 shifts at the Lighthouse Restaurant to make as much as I did from that one article. I guess it's time to get back to writing!

The Jan/Feb issue of *Power Boating Canada Magazine* has hit the newsstands. My first of a series of six articles, called "Diamond Lil Does the Loop", is in the issue. I am frustrated not to be able to see it.

Feb 9, 2009

The mooring field has been lonely, as we sat out the last three cold fronts that blew through West End. The conditions ranged from mildly unpleasant to downright miserable, so when a fourth front was predicted to be a nasty one, bringing higher winds for a longer period, we cut and ran. Or should I say, we attempted to cut and run?

I had just untied our lines from the mooring ball when the captain called me, and I knew by the sound of his voice that it wasn't good.

"I have no steering," he exclaimed, as he climbed down from the flybridge and attempted to steer from our lower navigation station, in the main cabin. The steering was as unresponsive downstairs as it had been upstairs.

Maneuvering *Diamond Lil* with only the transmission shifters, one of which only works in reverse, he gradually worked our way against the stiff wind back to the mooring ball, where we re-secured so he could investigate the problem. He discovered that the seal in the hydraulic steering pump up on the flybridge has broken. We have no choice but to stay put while we attempt to replace the part.

Feb 10, 2009

John set out bright and early this morning, in search of our replacement boat part. He rode in the cramped van, referred to here as a bus, as far as Coxen Hole. There he caught a *collectivo* to French Harbour, where all the automotive repair businesses and boatyards are located. He walked from one to another, checking for the part we needed. After eight stops, he moved on to Plan B.

Not being new to the island and knowing how slim the chances were of finding the part, he had a back-up plan. He had removed the T-cable connector, which joins the two steering systems, and was able to find someone to weld a piece into the opening for the flybridge steering cable, bypassing it so we could steer from downstairs.

If we were lucky, we would still have time to leave West End before the wind arrived. Once it does, the small cut in the reef becomes unnavigable.

Ten minutes after John returned, the small T was back in place and a few minutes later we were on our way. We drove from downstairs until we rounded the end of the island. Then we climbed upstairs and set course for French Harbour, at which point the autopilot was steering the boat. We just sat there looking at the hole where the steering wheel usually is and laughed. I was so relieved to be on our way. I really DID NOT want to spend another few days living in a blender.

Feb 13, 2009

It was a welcome change to be in French Harbour for a few days after two months in West End. However, after a few days, I became anxious to return. My late-life career at The Lighthouse Restaurant is on hold until business pick up. I've discovered it's far more lucrative to write for a living than to work for Honduran wages, so it's probably just as well.

We have learned a lot from being surrounded constantly by sailboats and decided, at least for now, not to replace our generator. Instead, we bought our first solar panel, which is 75 watts, and hooked it up in a temporary position. While we were in French Harbour, John bought some two by fours and material to install the panel on the roof of the flybridge, where it will capture the sun for most of the day.

Even with the panel installed temporarily on the bow, we are surprised how efficient it is. On a sunny day, which most days are here on the island, the one panel keeps our batteries charged.

Without our generator, we cannot use our electric stove or oven. For now, we are cooking on a Coleman propane stove and our grill and keeping our eyes open for a gas stove that might fit in the space where our electric stove is in our galley.

We make toast in a frying pan and warm up leftovers in a frying pan, like the old days before microwaves. Every day, we become more and more like the sailors surrounding us. We still run our decadent fridge/freezer and can make hot water by running our port-side engine once a day.

We will hopefully add more solar panels in time, that is if we can find them here. It is so much quieter to sit with our morning coffee without the generator running, not to mention the savings on the diesel fuel required to run it for three to four hours every day. Besides, there is an enormous hole in the side of it, and it does not run.

I am patiently waiting for the new screen for my laptop to be shipped to the island, so it can be installed. Today, we ordered the seal for the steering pump. It seems to be a constant challenge with this lifestyle, repairing or replacing things.

February 14, 2009

"Do you feel like checking out Carambola Botanical Gardens?" I asked the boss, over coffee this morning. "I've been dying to check it out ever since I chatted with Vanessa on the bus."

"Vanessa? What bus?" he asked, looking at me like I was crazy.

"Don't you remember me telling you about the girl I met on the bus on Christmas Eve day when I rode the *collectivo* into Coxen Hole to shop for you? Or, try to shop for you, is more like it," I reminded him.

"Vaguely, yeah, I suppose," he lied, badly.

"Ah, you're not going to drag me up another mountain, are you?" he whined. "I was planning to make the frames for the new solar panels today. I want to mount them on top of the flybridge, where they will catch more sun."

"Ah, come on honey. I've been reading about it in our tourist guide. Vanessa told me they have all kinds of exotic plants. I bet the view from up there is to die for. You can work on the frames later, or tomorrow."

"Whatever," he agreed.

Off we set, in the overstuffed *collectivo*.

Vanessa remembered me when John and I climbed out of the cramped little taxi.

"Hang on a second," I pleaded, as a group of tourists began their tour. "I need to snap a photo of the sign." John rolled his eyes as I jogged over to the road to snap a shot of the large sign.

"Take my picture," said Vanessa, as she posed in front of the group of tourists. A beautiful, white smile covered her face as she stood tall with her shoulders back and one arm on her hip. She wore a pink cotton skirt and a short-sleeved, black t-shirt. Her black hair was cut short and slicked back, almost man hair but on a cute female face.

"This way," called John. "I don't want to tag along on this geriatric tour. Let's just browse on our own."

"Sure," I agreed. "Look at this sign. There are two different nature trails we can hike."

"Let's just choose one," hubby said. "It's as hot as hell. We can come back another time and hike the other trail."

Snapping shots of pink lipstick palm trees, cinnamon trees, and a chocolate tree, we wound our way up the jungle trail. John looked like a child's toy next to an enormous Cahoon palm tree. As we slipped beneath the canopy, I commented that the temperature felt like it had dropped 20 degrees. The jungle trail led to the mountain trail, which was equally shaded and cool. Our reward at the top was a spectacular view of Anthony's Cay far below and the vast Caribbean Sea, stretching to the north as far as we could see.

Later, back at the boat, the captain built a frame for both the 75-watt solar panel and a small 10-watt panel that he picked up for next to nothing. The 75-watt panel gives us 4.7 amps of power. Our fridge uses 3.2 amps, leaving only 1.5 amps. The small 10-watt panel gives us an additional .5 watts or roughly 30% more power over and above what the fridge uses.

"Are you sure it's a good idea to mount it up there?" I asked as John outlined the plan. "Won't the weight of it ruin the canvas?"

"That's what the frame I am building is for. The panels will sit on it, not on the canvas."

"Well, won't the frame tear the canvas?" I insisted. I was concerned that the constant movement of the rocking boat would cause a problem.

"Just trust me, please!" he scolded, becoming slightly agitated.

"I'll climb up with this piece of wood and when I get up there, hand me the panel," he instructed.

Shocked to see him, with his intense fear of heights, scaling the narrow two by four, to the top of the flybridge on the rocking boat, I did as I was told. Quickly scaling the ladder to the flybridge, I guided the panel into place as he passed it to me.

This new location will give us several additional hours of sunlight on the panels. The temporary location, on the bow, is in full shade by mid-afternoon, when the sun is shining on the back of the boat. Except for rare occasions when a storm approaches, the predominant winds blow from the east. Since we are swinging on an anchor, we also face east, with the back deck facing west, perfect for watching the sunset in the evening.

March 3, 2009

Life changes quickly from one moment to the next when you live on a boat. I was wandering down the sandy, little seaside road in West End on Sunday morning on my way to Charlie's Internet Café. I had just been told that there was work for me at the Lighthouse Restaurant, as tourism is picking up here on the island.

"Are you guys staying for the big blow or heading out?" asked a neighbor from the anchorage as I passed him on the road.

"What blow?" I asked, thereby admitting our neglect to check the weather, surely the gravest sin for a boater.

"Thirty knots, coming from the northwest and west. The kind of weather that tends to throw boats up on the beach," he explained.

He has lived on his boat here in West End for ten years and has counted 250 boats drag anchor during that time. That is quite a hobby, I thought to myself, counting boats that drag anchor.

I hurried to the internet café to confirm this bit of bad news. What horrible timing. Just as I am called back to work, we must leave West End. Luckily, I warned Johnna that I cannot return to work until this Thursday because we are expecting company on the boat.

We picked up several 5-gallon bottles of drinking water, which is easier to do in West End than French Harbour. We shopped for produce, which is fresher here than in French Harbour, despite the somewhat modern grocery store there.

Within an hour of hearing about the impending harsh weather, we were heading east, battling the choppy waves which covered our boat with a scum of salt. The captain was not happy with the conditions. I was not happy leaving West End. I didn't call for the bloody cold front, I barked at him.

By 4:00 pm, we were swinging peacefully at anchor in the beautiful anchorage beside Little French Cay. My favorite spot was open, the prettiest spot in the anchorage, I believe. By 5:00 pm, we were sitting in town, scarfing down delicious Pizza Inn pizza.

We took advantage of the calm before the storm the next day to do some snorkeling. All the boaters were doing the same thing, expecting harsh weather to limit the in-water activities once the front arrived.

The cold front arrived at precisely 12:30 a.m. on Monday morning. We sat up and watched for dragging boats. If it's going to happen, it's usually just as the front hits. Satisfied that all was well, we returned to bed. At 4:00 a.m., I was still awake, listening to the wind howl and the creaks and thumps that accompany it.

Our 90-day visas are up on March 9th. This morning, the captain set off to Coxen Hole with our passports in hand, to apply for a 90-day extension, while I stayed on the boat to write.

Several hours later he returned, hot and bothered. The renewal fee of $100.00 US per person from last year has increased to $225.00 US per person this year, a shocking increase. John discovered this after waiting for most of the afternoon for the immigration officer to return from a meeting. Waiting is a way of life here. The captain is much better at waiting than when I met him years ago, but he does have his limits.

The following day we did some investigating and found someone who would renew the visas for $100.00 each

and were thrilled to save the $250.00. We are here for
another 90 days at least!

March 4, 2009

We first met Jim and Jeanie Long two years ago, during
the first hurricane season we spent in the Rio Dulce.
Diamond Lil was docked two slips away from their boat,
Oasis, at Mario's Marina. They spent the following
summer in Roatan, as we did. They returned to the Rio
the next summer, as we did. Their boat is still there, but
they have come by bus from Guatemala to La Ceiba, and
then by ferry, from La Ceiba, on the mainland of
Honduras, to Roatan, to visit us.

John met them on the shore in French Harbour and
brought them through the busy anchorage at Little
French Cay, to *Diamond Lil*, where they would spend a
couple of days with us.

I waved at them from the aft deck, as they got closer.
Both wore light jackets, odd for this climate. They must
have been bundled up for the effective air conditioning
on the ferry, or yacht, as the locals refer to it.

Jim wore a huge smile as he waved back. He wore a
bright blue and purple tie-dyed bandana tied over his
head, wrap-around sunglasses, and a sporty mustache.
He had on short pants, a white undershirt, and a short-
sleeved cotton shirt with a giant leaping sailfish
pattern. Over that, he had on a grey fleece jacket with
his eyeglasses hanging from his neck.

Jeanie had on white cotton shorts and a white cotton hoodie zipped up to her neck. Her long, blonde hair was piled high on top of her head in a big bun. She wore snap-on sunglasses, also on a chain around her neck, making sure they didn't end up in the drink.

Mar 5, 2009

There is an unspoken rule that the head (toilet) on your boat will work until guests arrive. I woke this morning to the sight of a man running through my cabin wearing nothing but a pair of boxer shorts. He held a dripping mop in his hand as he dashed out to the aft deck.

I looked over to see the captain still sound asleep beside me. As I sat up and wiped my fuzzy eyes, I realized that it was Jim on the back deck with the mop.

"Sorry," he whispered. "I was trying to be quiet, so I didn't wake you. We seem to have broken your head and I've been trying to clean up some water from the floor. Geez, this is embarrassing."

"It's ok," said John, as he appeared on the scene. "There was a hairline crack in it, so don't feel too bad. It was bound to happen one day soon."

"All the same, we feel like a couple of real asses," he laughed. "Let me know what I can do to help you fix it."

"It's ok," said John. "I've been putting it off, so you did me a favor."

"He can fix anything," I said, trying to make them feel better. "That's why I married him."

Not long after we had waved good-bye to our good friends, the captain had his plumber's hat on and was grunting and groaning as he attempted to fit his body into the tiny space in the head to repair the leak. Before long, the head was leak-free and as good as new.

March 11, 2009

Our boat company has departed, and we are back in the anchorage at West End.

During our visit to French Harbour, we heard through the coconut telegraph that several boaters are using mobile broadband USB modems to get an internet signal on their boats.

The thought of having internet service on the boat has me excited. It will work anywhere we can get a Tigo signal, so it will work when we are anchored offshore. It will even work when we are underway between the Bay Islands.

I placed a call to Paradise Computers in Coxen Hole.

"Yes, we are getting some modems in next week," the man on the phone told me.

Having heard this line before, we asked Stephen, who provides a successful laundry service for the boaters in French Harbour, if he knew where we could find one. He is a wealth of information about island life.

Stephen checked with his contact on the mainland, who offered to bring some modems to the island on the ferry. We could have it in two days, by Friday, he told us. That means we could have it in time for my birthday, on Saturday!

March 13, 2009

Stephen spent the entire day trying to get in touch with his friend on the mainland. Our emotions were up and down like a toilet seat all day, as the delivery was on and off and on and off. Traipsing around Coxen Hole all afternoon had exhausted us. We returned to the boat, feeling disappointed.

It was 8:00 pm by the time we received the call from Stephen. We loaded our laptop into the dinghy and set off across the black harbor. He would meet us onshore in West End to install the modem on the laptop.

The installation was not successful and feeling downtrodden once again, we returned to the boat, as Stephen left for home on his scooter, to try to solve the problem.

Not long after we were settled on the boat, our phone rang. Stephen had solved the problem. We would meet in West End at 7:30 a.m. the next morning.

March 14, 2009

At 7:00 in the morning, the phone rang. True to his word, Stephen was in town, waiting for us. We had been up for a while, so we hopped in the dinghy and headed for shore. This time, the unit was installed successfully. Now we have internet wherever we receive a cell phone signal, both here and in the Rio, which means internet service ON THE BOAT! This is a major improvement in communications for us, as well as much more pleasure and entertainment. What a great birthday gift!

West End is one of the most inspirational places we have ever spent time in. I feel like I have stepped from reality into the pages of a novel, set in a funky little town full of ex-pats, beach bums, divers, Spaniards from the Honduran mainland, tourists from all over the world, boaters, and locals.

Beauty surrounds us. There are many days when I am so content on the boat that I don't even get off.

The large, black hole where a piece blew out of our generator

Cheryl and Miguel

The Lighthouse Restaurant in West End

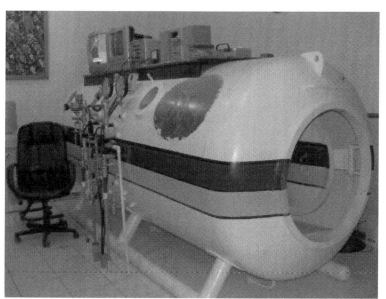

The hyperbaric chamber at Anthony's Key Resort

John, driving from the flybridge using the autopilot

The sign for Carambola Botanical Gardens, just outside West End

Vanessa, a tour guide at Carambola Gardens

View of Anthony's Key Resort from above at Carambola Gardens

John, on the bow, about to mount his new panels

Two Solar Panels mounted on the roof of *Diamond Lil*

The anchorage at Little French Cay

Stephen, installing our new internet modem in West End

John, picking up Jim and Jeanie Long from shore in French Harbour

Jeanie, stocking up on Miracle Whip before returning to the Rio

Chapter 3

March 25, 2009

I've been called back to work at the Lighthouse Restaurant. Their business has picked up. The tips have improved as well. The work is hard but enjoyable. There is never a dull moment between working, writing, painting, swimming, snorkeling, fishing, walking, and dancing like fools in the West End bars at night.

Mike, or Miguel, as he prefers to be called, buzzed us from his cell phone as he and Cheryl passed *Diamond Lil* in their sailing vessel, *Let it Be*, this morning. They had left Guanaja at the break of day and were headed for Utila, the westernmost of the three Bay Islands. Their route brought them directly past the anchorage at West End.

"Well, was it as great as we told you? Did you love it?" I asked Miguel.

"Oh man, I think it is my favorite island ever," replied Miguel zealously, echoing our sentiments from last year's visit. "There's a big party for Hansito's 50th birthday," added Miguel. "I wish we could have stayed, but we are meeting friends in Belize."

Guanaja is the easternmost of the three main Bay Islands, with the smallest population, and the fewest tourists. Hansito is the owner of the Manati Bar and Restaurant, a popular hangout for both gringos and locals in Guanaja. John and I first discovered the

Manati on Hansito's birthday, last year, on our first visit to that island.

We were greeted like royalty on that first visit, treated to a free German meal in honor of the birthday boy, and made to feel welcome the way all visitors to the Manati are. This year's bash was going to be the biggest party the island had ever seen, Miguel told us. Three hundred people were expected, with many of them flying in from Germany.

The wheels started turning in my head at lightning speed. The Lighthouse Restaurant only needed me for a few more shifts until another server returned from vacation. We had intended to head straight for Guanaja when we left the Rio. Somehow, we got stuck in Roatan, mainly West End. What sticky harbors these are!

"What do you say?" I pleaded with John, as I laid out my plan.

"We'll see," he grunted, as he buried his head in his novel.

I knew he was sold on the plan when he set aside his novel and began to thumb through our cruising guides. That was my sign. My captain is a quiet guy, so I have had to learn to read these subtle signals. He doesn't open a cruising guide unless he has decided to go. YES!

We began our series of trips into West End for supplies; groceries, gasoline for the dinghy, and phone cards for both phone and internet. There is tasty coffee to be had in West End, but not on the island of Guanaja, we learned last year. Armed with three large bags of coffee and a few coveted items, we were off.

We had studied the weather reports all week. Conditions were not ideal, but we noticed a couple of brief weather windows. We would travel part-way on Thursday afternoon and the rest of the way either Friday or Saturday morning, depending on the wind.

So it's off to sea, off to sea. Here we come, Guanaja!

March 30, 2009

Thrilled to be back in Guanaja, I set to work on a painting of the Manati Restaurant, decorated for Hansito's 50th birthday party. I asked John to run me over to the restaurant in our dinghy as soon as I finished my coffee, so I could snap a photo of the blue streamers dancing in the wind. I had no blank canvas, so I found an old paint-by-numbers set and painted over top of it. Necessity is the mother of invention when you're in the middle of nowhere.

Warm, fuzzy memories from our times at the Manati when we stayed here last year have had me excited about this party ever since Miguel sailed past us in West End. The party is this afternoon, so I will have to work quickly.

Mar 31, 2009

The docking area was thick with boats of all sizes as we wove our trusty dinghy through the obstacle course of vessels and tied to shore. Children kicked a soccer ball around the lawn in front of the building. Hundreds of blue and green balloons hung from the ceiling. Shiny blue and silver streamers danced in the island breeze, many with toy red motorbikes hanging from them.

Happy Birthday banners in bright colors were abundant, as were giant blue and silver number 50's.

A group of local ex-pats entertained the crowd with music reminiscent of a German beer garden. I filmed Klaus, with his long, blonde hair, tied back in a ponytail, playing his bass guitar. I filmed a man wearing a jaunty beret, playing the accordion. There was a Tom Selleck lookalike on guitar and an intense man playing the keyboard. I filmed a rakish couple dancing to the music. He wore a straw cowboy hat, wire-rimmed glasses, and a tank top. She had short, wispy blonde hair, and wore a black, sleeveless cotton dress.

Annette, who with her husband, Klaus, manages the business, buzzed about the place, tending bar and clearing tables. She darted in and out of the kitchen, a blur of activity. She is a small woman, short and very trim. She favors full length, flowing sundresses, which she normally wears without a bra. I envied her the ability to dress in such a cool way in this steamy climate. Her long, medium-brown hair is parted on the side and pulled back in a ponytail. She glowed – that is she was working hard, dashing in and out of a hot kitchen, and it showed. The smile never left her face for a moment though, and I could tell she took pride in the work she did.

A woman sang a slow version of *Happy Birthday to You*, Marilyn Monroe style, while Hansito downed an enormous Weizen glassful of beer, to the cheers of the crowd. He was tall and thin, with somewhat sharp features. Despite having half a century under his belt, his hair was still dark, almost black, and only beginning to recede, ever so slightly.

His five o'clock shadow, more like a few days old, was also still dark, as were his bushy eyebrows. He had been wearing a light blue t-shirt when we arrived, but I noticed he had changed into a grey one with an Aéropostale logo across the front. The heat, I reasoned, had been the cause of the change. Perhaps it was spillage from the enormous beer glass.

Crowds of people milled about inside the restaurant, and all over the ample, neatly manicured grounds. A makeshift bar was set up outside to help accommodate the throngs of well-wishers.

I filmed John, standing at the little outdoor bar, watching a woman refill our white plastic cups with rum and coke. She held both cups in one hand, and the bottle of *Flor de Cana* in the other. In went the rum, more and more of it and finally, the splash of coke that passes for mix.

I filmed the long lineup of revelers, using their empty plastic plates as fans in the afternoon heat as they stood waiting to have them filled with roast pork and a wide selection of delicious, German side dishes.

The crowd was well behaved, considering that the festivities had started around noon. A free bar is an open invitation to possible mayhem around here. Fun was had by everyone, and Hansito loved his painting of the Manati, decorated for his special day.

April 5, 2009

The island of Guanaja itself is approximately 25 kilometers long by four kilometers wide. However, about 80% of the population does not live on this main island, but rather on Bonacca, just a short distance from the main island. Bonacca appears to be one small island from the distance, but it began as two small cays that were joined over time.

Bonacca is also known as Guanaja Town. Usually, the locals refer to it is as the cay. The cay is home to about 8,000 people, living in an area of roughly 10 acres. Apparently, there are more people per square mile living here than in Hong Kong.

In places, the original narrow canals on the cay run between the buildings, but most have been filled in with cement and made into narrow little concrete walkways.

At first glance, Bonacca is one giant maze, but after spending a month here last year, we know our way around. Narrow pathways weave in and out between buildings, around corners, over canals, and end up in countless dead ends. Most stores are not marked with signs, nor are any of the little strips of pavement that pass for streets. Most homes have open windows and doors, providing an up-close and personal glimpse into the cay-dwellers' lives. Some of it is not so pretty. I have witnessed the odd rat, scurrying in the shadows inside, as I pass by these modest homes.

Bonacca is a stilt town, as other settlements in the islands are, but the stilts are anchored on a submerged shoal. Densely clustered wooden buildings, painted the colors of tropical fruit, give the island a shimmery, mirage-like appearance from a distance.

The cay is where we go, by dinghy, from our anchorage in El Bight, when we need anything. All the banks, shops, bars, and restaurants are there. Tony, our boat boy from last year, showed up one day while we were on the cay. He offered to watch our dinghy while we shopped and carried our bags for us, in exchange for a small tip.

We were as happy to see him as he was to see us. We invited him to join us for lunch, but he would not accept our offer. We bought him a cold drink, and I shared my deep-fried plantains, while we caught up on the news since last year.

Tony is saving the tip money he makes, helping gringos like us, for a new pair of flip flops, which he referred to as slippers. He was thrilled to tell us that he was going fishing with the men for the first time. They were heading for the Cayman banks. All he needs to do is tell his teacher that he is going to the banks, and he gets out of school. However, he must take his homework out on the fishing boat to do while he is away. I asked how long he planned to go to school and how old he was. He said he wasn't sure how long he would go to school, as his father is no longer living. When I asked him when his birthday was, he didn't know. We couldn't believe it. He thinks he is 13 but isn't sure what day he was born.

April 9, 2009

We bade farewell to Guanaja, after 11 days. I had mixed feelings about leaving the natural unspoiled beauty of the island. Change is coming, and as locals bragged about the new roads being built on the island and cars arriving, I couldn't help but feel the loss of something special, a tranquil haven where no traffic exists.

The outboard motor for our dinghy stopped running while we were in Guanaja. A mechanic, who came highly recommended, determined that we needed a new head gasket, so we'll have one shipped to Roatan. Also, Mom and Dad Wood offered to ship us an old small motor they aren't using, for which we are very thankful.

John told me about an advertisement he read in the Chisme Vindicator, a Rio Dulce website that we follow. The ad is for free dockage and electricity in Oak Ridge Harbour, Roatan, in exchange for feeding two dogs and watching the property while the owner travels home to the US. So, with no outboard, and no generator we thought what the heck, let's try something different.

It's back to Roatan for *Diamond Lil* and crew.

Dressed for work at the Lighthouse Restaurant in West End

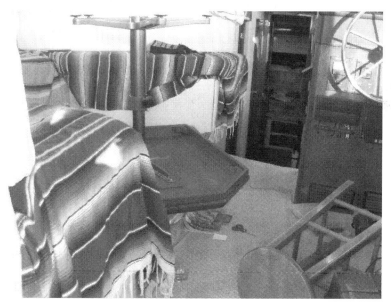

Result of the rough passage between Roatan and Guanaja

The Manati Restaurant and Bar in El Bight, Guanaja

Boat parking at Hansito's 50th birthday party at the Manati

Florian, carving the roast pig

Hansito's well attended 50th birthday party at the Manati

Hansito, drinking from his Weizen glass

John, with *Diamond Lil* anchored in El Bight, Guanaja

Chapter 4

April 9, 2009

"John, I see a turd," I yelled out, as he edged *Diamond Lil* up to the dock at Oak Ridge Point. Looking over to the house, I saw Mr. Larry, from Jonesville Marina, sitting with Joe, the owner of the property.

"Don't be ridiculous," shouted John back at me. "It's a bloody stick. Try paying attention to getting the boat on the dock, will you?"

"Some stick. It has corn stuck in it. It's a turd. You brought me from beautiful Guanaja, to tie to shore in water with turds floating in it!"

I was still resentful of our decision to come here.

"One night," I added. "You promised that if I don't like it after one night, you won't insist on staying."

"Yes, dear," he barked. "We've been over and over this. I can't fix the outboard while we are anchored. We have no generator. I need some time at a dock. It's only for three months. We'll be gone before you know it."

Once we had *Diamond Lil* settled in her new home, Joe invited us to join him and Mr. Larry for a drink. He really hoped that we would stay, he told us. Mr. Larry had given us a high recommendation.

"If we enjoy it here tonight, we will commit to three months," I told him.

Joe was a little less than average in height, with a slim build, ice blue eyes behind wire-rimmed glasses and medium brown hair, cut short. A neatly trimmed mustache completed a boyish sort of face.

"It's quite a tight-knit neighborhood, here on the Point," said Joe. "I hope you don't mind, but I've invited a couple of neighbors over for the cocktail hour. It's important that they like the people who are staying here, and vice versa."

Back at the boat, as we showered and changed, I chuckled as I told John that it felt like we were being interviewed by the neighbors for the property sitting job.

The Point is a long, narrow peninsula separated from the town of Oak Ridge proper by a channel about 400-feet wide. A sandy path that runs along the shoreline leads to a small footbridge that connects the Point to the main island. Directly across the water from us is the back of a yellow brick building. 'Hessie's Supermarket,' reads the sign in the window.

The sound of music, wafting across the water from Hessie's, brings back warm fuzzy feelings. I have always enjoyed docking the boat in places where music is in the air. The distance is perfect. It's not too loud, and the selection is wonderful.

"I really love this music," I said to John. "So far, I like it here."

Sure enough, Miss Sandy and Miss Donna, two of the neighbors, opened the little wooden gate at the side of the property, strolled along the grassy path and climbed up the steps to join us for drinks on the veranda, which wraps around two sides of the house.

Miss Sandy is a real-life Southern belle, or should I say she was one in her earlier days. She is a handsome woman, with dark blue eyes. Her medium-brown hair is swept up and piled loosely on top of her head. She wore long, navy blue cotton pants and a long-sleeved cotton blouse, buttoned up to the neck. On her feet, she wore old-fashioned, inexpensive, slip-on sneakers, with socks. This seems most unusual in a place where flip flops are the norm.

She grew up in New Orleans, Louisiana, and her fair complexion looks like she did not leave her bonnet behind. Her thick, Southern drawl has stayed with her all these years, as well. Her daddy, she told us, brought her to Tegucigalpa, the capital of Honduras, when she was a young woman. Daddy traveled in some well-heeled circles of businessmen and diplomats. Miss Sandy, a Roatan resident for over 30 years, has some grand tales to tell.

Miss Donna is shorter, with short, greyish-brown hair and a round, cheery face. Dark brown eyes behind wire-rimmed glasses are framed by delicate laugh lines. She seems a little quieter and more laid back than Miss Sandy, who did most of the talking. She is from North Carolina, she told us, as we made introductions. Her accent is much more subdued than Miss Sandy's.

"Have y'all met Miss Jessie, yet?" Miss Sandy asked.

"No, we just arrived a couple of hours ago," I said.

"She lives next door," Donna said, as she walked to the end of the balcony, closest to the seaside, and pointed at a small, white wooden house. It, like most houses on the island, was built on posts, above the ground.

"Most people call her Aunt Jessie," said Sandy. "She will be 85 years old next month. I'm sure you will meet her soon. Her daughter, Alana, lives up on the hill above town, but she comes to see her Mama often."

"That reminds me. Alana will be dropping by one day soon," added Joe. "She's coming to take Jip's stitches out. She was spayed last week." Jip is one of the two dogs on the property.

Once the meet the neighbors, happy hour session had come to an end, we bade Joe and the ladies good night, stepped down from the veranda, and strolled the few feet across the patchy lawn to *Diamond Lil*, waiting on the dock.

Here we are in our new home, tied to a dock, plugged in, running computers and fans and all kinds of decadent electronic gadgets. We can use our stove and microwave and toaster and vacuum for the first time in a few months. John can work on the motor onshore in peace and not drive me crazy dripping oil all over the boat.

We have a beautiful, fenced piece of property all to ourselves. It is situated on the far end of Oak Ridge Point. We can snorkel from a small dock on the seaside of the property, which is very close to the reef. There are schools of fish and lobsters in shallow water that we can wade in to catch. We may be here for a month. We may be here for three months, but this is where we are for now.

There is even a washing machine, which may be sold shortly, but before it is, I am going to wash my own clothes for the first time since we left Mario's Marina, a year and a half ago. I can't wait! After scrubbing sheets and towels in our bathtub with a very limited water supply, I will never complain about doing laundry in a real washing machine again.

We have an internet signal through HughesNet. Although we have our new internet modem, we won't have to buy time for it while we are here, a savings of $12.00US/week or $48.00/month.

Our limited duties include feeding the two dogs, named Jip and Chiquita. Chiquita has the shape, coat texture, and coloring of a husky but is smaller. She has been known to bite anyone who tries to come on the property. People are quite proud of dogs that bite here on the island.

Jip is medium-sized, short-haired, with a reddish-brown coat, and looks to be part hound. She is a recent addition to the property, replacing the previous dog, which was poisoned. Not Chiquita, though, we were told. As well as being heralded as a biter, she is poison-proof.

April 10, 2009

The wind is howling under a full, orange moon,
illuminating the white caps out on the ocean. John
asked me just now if he should turn on the VHF radio,
so we can listen to the poor souls dragging anchor down
in French Harbour. That's because we are tied securely
to shore at our little private resort here on Oak Ridge
Point. At least that is what it feels like. After four
months living at anchor, the shore is a treat, believe me!

I'm sure most people wouldn't find clothes hanging on a
line photo-worthy. However, after two years of handing
our dirty laundry over to strangers and getting it back,
damp, and having it turn greyer and dingier over time,
it was heaven for me to wash our own clothes. I soaked
our dingy, grey garments in Blanco, the magic formula
they use on the island that makes clothes look great
when washed in cold water. The sight of my laundry,
flapping in the breeze, was a comforting sight.

John dragged the outboard motor into *La Feets,* which
serves as a combination laundry room, workshop, and
storage shed. Yes, the shed has a name. After tearing
the motor apart, he discovered that all we need is a
head gasket. He searched the internet and found one for
sale in Florida. The regular price is $14.00 US. It is on
sale for $3.00. With the cost of shipping at $6.00, it is on
the way to Roatan for under $10.00.

We wander around this large property and lose each
other, literally. It's comical, after years of always being
within sight and sound of each other on the boat. We

poked around in the mangroves along the walkway to town yesterday. I dug out two old-looking bottles and cleaned them up. I am on a mission to find some for Ronald, the painter in West End, who said he would trade me for some blank canvases that he buys from the mainland.

"There is a new grocery store up there," Joe had told us when we first arrived and asked about shopping in town. He pointed up, way up, across the bight, high in the hills. "There is a short cut that takes you right into their parking lot," he said.

Off we set on our mission, first rowing across the canal to pick up a five-gallon jug of drinking water. How much further could it be, we wondered, as we continued to walk. On and on we walked. Soon the road began to lead uphill – way uphill! The store hadn't looked quite so far from over at the Point. The short cut was not very short, nor was the newly opened grocery store open yet.

The view of the Point and the little canal leading through the small cut between Pandy Town and Oak Ridge Cay was spectacular, however.

"I can't quite get the shot because of the trees in the way," I complained to John, as I scaled to the highest possible point.

"If I can just get up into that tree a little bit, to the bottom branches, I think I can get the shot," I said.

"Ah geez. Here, hand me the camera. I'll climb up the tree. The things I do for you!"

Exhausted from the long walk through town to the not-so-short short-cut, and soaked with perspiration, we hailed the first taxi we saw and rode back to our dinghy, which was still where we had left it, at Hessie's dock.

One of the first things we did after arriving dockside here at the Point, once *Diamond Lil* was plugged into the *luz*, or electricity as we know it, was to disassemble the ugly, old, rusty Coleman two-burner camp stove that has been sitting on top of our electric stove in the galley for the past few months. We hauled the large propane tank for the barbeque back to the perfect, out-of-the-way spot on the flybridge, where we usually keep it. The only place to keep it close enough to the galley to hook up to the Coleman stove, but not in the way, was in our spare bedroom, so I was thrilled to have it removed.

We had just returned to our boat, after being invited to a neighbor's house for a Good Friday cocktail, and were about to bake some coconut shrimp in the oven, when the town went black and became instantly quiet. The Good Friday celebration, which had been in full swing, ground to a halt. We spotted the odd bonfire along the shore and heard car speakers playing music, but at a fraction of the volume of the previous festivities.

As boatloads of families passed us, returning home in the darkness of the night, we sighed and climbed up to the flybridge. We pulled down the old and rusty, but useful propane stove, and hauled the big tank right back to where it had been before we so wisely decided to put it away.

Now, a week later, we have returned to the old set up. "No luz" is a common expression here. The situation is far better than it was last year when power outages occurred almost daily, but this past week, during *Semana Santa,* or Holy Week, we have experienced several outages.

Two nights ago, I had just taken my first dozen cupcakes out of the oven (it only holds that many), made our tea, and put the second dozen cupcakes in the oven, when the luz went out. The fish enjoyed the second batch of half-baked cupcakes. This outage was caused by a fire on a pole half-way down the Point, and the power was out from 7:00 pm until 10:00 a.m. the next morning.

Last night, we managed to roast a chicken in the oven without losing the power. Because we only have 15-amp service to the boat, we cannot use the oven and burners or the oven and the microwave at the same time. So, the ugly, old propane stove once again is a part of the family.

I boiled potatoes and steamed veggies on it while roasting the chicken in the electric oven. Then I shut off the oven and warmed some leftover stuffing in the microwave, juggling my veggies, potatoes, and gravy on two burners. When it was all ready, I turned the oven back on broil for a couple of minutes to heat and brown the chicken.

Voila. We enjoyed a delicious chicken dinner with all the fixings; broccoli and carrots from French Harbour, green beans from West End, and chicken and potatoes from Oak Ridge. It takes a lot of shopping to pull together a meal that is not chicken, rice and beans, believe me. With cupcakes and hot, decaf tea for dessert, and we were happy campers.

The public transit is inexpensive on the island. We have made a couple of trips to French Harbour and one to West End. First, we went to the bank machine to withdraw cash. Then, we picked up our mail that John's daughter, Samantha, so kindly forwarded to Roatan Air, the courier service we use. There is a post office in Coxen Hole, but we have heard horror stories about mail arriving years after it was sent, or not at all. Finally, we shopped for groceries at Eldon's Supermarket, which wouldn't impress anyone back in the first world, but it is loaded compared to the stores in Oak Ridge.

We visited friends in West End and chose from the best selection of fruit and vegetables on the island, which is sold from the back of pick-up trucks along the street. We dined on good old American burgers and fries at Rocket Burger and headed home. The bus ride each way was two hours long. One bus took us from Oak Ridge, through the Garifuna town of Punta Gorda, which lies on the north coast and down island to Coxen Hole. It is a scenic trip, but I was on the shore side of the bus and not the beachside, so I didn't get many pictures. Coming home, my memory card was full, therefore I didn't get pictures then either, even of the perfect sunset over the flat calm water.

The bus driver drove so slowly that John and I joked that we could walk alongside and keep up. John suspected that it had something to do with the loose steering. We sat in the back seat and listened to the windshield washer motor run the entire way, regardless of the fact there were no actual window washers on the bus.

From Coxen Hole, another bus took us to West End, a trip we have taken many times. The first bus ride, about an hour and a half long, cost us 35 lempiras each, or about $1.75. The second bus trip, about half an hour-long, cost 20 lempiras each or about a dollar. Bus is a vague term. Sometimes it is a bus, sometimes a van, always with a lot of creaks and grinds and strange noises. Unlike in Canada, where vehicles need to be safety certified, here if it has wheels and rolls, you're on the road!

Yesterday, we walked from the Point, through the town of Oak Ridge, and around the end of the bight to Pandy Town, which we can see across the water from the boat. It is a predominantly black community where mostly English is spoken. We found one surprisingly well-stocked store, where we plan to shop once we get our wheels back. By our wheels, of course, I mean our dinghy. Without it, we are lost in this water-based community. There are water taxis available, but nothing beats our own dinghy for exploring the area.

Mom and Dad Wood have shipped us a 2.2-horsepower motor and a gasket for the 15-horsepower motor is on the way.

The music has come back on at the grocery store across the canal from us. Whenever they are open, providing we have luz, the music is on. Sometimes it's reggae, sometimes it's Spanish music, and this morning it was mellow gringo 60's type stuff. It adds a festive feel to the place. However, over on this side of the narrow waterway, there is still no luz. A mere 400 feet from us, they have power. Here, we have no power!

April 22, 2009

The people of Honduras, like those in Guatemala, celebrate almost as many holidays as there are days of the year. We were in the Roatan Air office yesterday, picking up the replacement head gasket for our 15-horsepower outboard motor. I asked when the next shipment was due because our 2.2-horsepower motor is on its way from Florida.

"Our next shipment is due either later today or tomorrow," said the clerk.

"We won't be open tomorrow, though," he said. "It's a holiday."

"What holiday is it?" I asked.

"I don't know," he answered, in broken English, giggling with nervous tension.

Each of the customers standing at the counter with us had a comment, but none of them knew what holiday it was either.

When we returned to the boat, I googled official Honduran holidays and it's not official at all, but an unofficial Honduran holiday – "International Earth Day". Silly me. We celebrate the same holiday in Canada.

Most *tiendas*, or small stores, are still open, but Roatan Air, also known as Rasta Airlines, is closed for Earth Day.

With the gasket in hand, we walked a couple of miles from the Roatan Air office into French Harbour to check out the new Eldon's Sun Supermarket. WOW! The new building is about three times the size of the old one and has a much larger selection. We browsed along with curious islanders, gringos, and the boaters that you find around French Harbour.

We were like kids in a candy store. We found items we hadn't seen on the island before, items we took for granted back in the land of plenty. We found green relish, mushrooms, romaine lettuce, a large selection of bakery items, Borden cheese, and Tylenol.

After bartering with several taxi drivers for the half-hour ride back to Oak Ridge, we paid 100 lempiras or $5.00 for both of us. Back at the dock, we piled our wares into the dinghy, which we had left tied up at Hessie's store, and rowed across to the boat for the last time.

Captain Fix-It had the gasket into the motor in a matter of minutes,die and we were off for a ride. Living in the Venice of the Caribbean without a boat has been agonizing for us. Hole in the Wall was our destination, as we buzzed through Oak Ridge in our rubber raft. Under the small footbridge, we went, past the little community of Lucy Point, past the huge shrimp and lobster boats moored in front of Jonesville, past Puky's Restaurant, and into the bight in front of the community of Blue Rock.

As we neared the Hole in the Wall dock, we were greeted by the bow-legged old hound dog, one of the resident pets. His drool covered face looked directly into mine, as I scrambled up onto the dock to tie the boat.

The place looked much the same as it had last year. Built out over the water, it was a bare-bones structure, complete with rickety dock boards that tilted to one side when you walked, even before you had your first rum punch. A mural in the form of brick siding was painted on the walls. From the tin roof above hung a collection of old, faded t-shirts and ball-caps, autographed by rum-soaked tourists from all over the world. Perched on a small table against the kitchen wall was a basket of large, fat, cigars, which were free for the taking.

It was Sunday when the famous all you can eat buffet was served. From the far corner of the building, came the smoky aroma of beef, grilling on an oil drum barbeque. Two teenage boys tended a huge pot full of steaming lobster tails.

I peered into the kitchen, where I found Mr. Bob, Harry, and Dwayne, standing together at the counter, intent on their work. Mr. Bob, the owner of Hole in the Wall, was an imposing man in his sixties, with snow-white hair, a mustache, and a snow-white beard. His ruddy, tan complexion suggested a sun-filled life. He wore a white Hole in the Wall tank top and clenched between his smiling lips was one of his signature fat cigars.

Standing behind Mr. Bob was Harry, one of his two sidekicks. Harry was shorter than Mr. Bob, with a small, round face, salt and pepper hair, mustache and beard. He wore a short-sleeved, black cotton shirt.

Dwayne was standing behind Bob and Harry, slightly bent over the counter, pouring a drink. He was a little taller than Harry, with a thick head of brown hair and big brown eyes. His mouth was a mere slit between a massive brown beard and a thick, brown mustache. His nose was wide and flat like he had done a little boxing earlier in life. Dwayne had on a short-sleeved cotton shirt, with a black background covered in a brightly colored Mexican style pattern of chili peppers. When he walked, his legs were almost as bowed as the old hound dog. He was a blacksmith back in the real world, I had learned last year.

Harry and Dwayne lived on their sailboats, which were docked directly beside the restaurant. We chatted with them over a rum punch, as the late afternoon sun lit up the verdant jungle across the bight. Not a single structure marred the picture-perfect scenery.

Feeling warm and fuzzy, from finding our old watering hole still open and thriving, we returned to the Point and backed into our boathouse. What a luxury it is to have a two-door, fully lit, dry boathouse. Our days of baling out our dinghy after it rains are over! The added security of having Chiquita sleep in there, at night, is an added bonus. The coconut telegraph is alive and well.

"That dog, she bites!" we hear, over and over, as we meet people around town.

May 4, 2009

I can't believe that it was a month ago today that we tied to the dock here at Oak Ridge Point. If the breeze stopped blowing, we would die from the heat, but fortunately, it never stops blowing. *Diamond Lil* is a conversation piece in her new home at the Point.

There is an old man in town who just shakes his head every time he sees us and says, "A powerboat, man you guys are an oddity."

He introduces us to anyone who will listen and tells them that we are the oddity around here, being in a powerboat. That's us, odd. The whole fricking town is odd if you ask me.

We stopped in at a little bar across the bay called The Blue Bayou. John ordered a rum and coke.

"No ron, solo coca," the woman told us. John walked a few feet down the road to a store and bought a little bottle of rum.

"Tiene un vaso de hielo?" I asked the same woman, hoping to add ice to John's drink.

"No hielo," she said – no ice.

John choked down his warm rum and coke, his rum bottle sitting in front of him on the table. I felt like we have stepped onto a movie set in some shady Banana Republic.

Mr. Joe, coming to greet us as we arrived at Oak Ridge Point, Roatan

Diamond Lil, docked at Oak Ridge Point, Roatan. Boathouse to the right.

The bus we took from Oak Ridge to Coxen Hole.

School children, traveling to school in the municipal boat.

John was thrilled to have the dinghy back in the water.

Harry's old bow-legged dog at Hole in the Wall

Mr. Bob (front), Harry (middle), and Dwayne (back)

Abogado, enjoying the all you can eat Buffet at Hole in the Wall

John, working on our outboard motor in "La Feets"

John, at Hole in the Wall, with one of Bob's famous free cigars

Chapter 5

The whistle from across the canal that meant that John was back from his down-island shopping excursion came way too soon.

Oh no, I thought to myself. He must have forgotten his wallet or something.

"What did you forget?" I asked him as I eased our dinghy up to the dock beside Hessie's store, to pick him up.

As he scrambled down into the dinghy, I noticed that he wasn't carrying a single bag. Normally, he returns laden with items that are unavailable in Oak Ridge.

"Three shots. You wouldn't believe it!" was all he said, pointing across the canal to *Diamond Lil,* meaning let's go.

The details tumbled out in bits and pieces as he began to tell me his tale. He had ridden as far as the Jackson Plaza, between French Harbour and Los Fuertes. That is where the closest bank machine is that accepts our Canadian debit card. He was about to turn the corner when Stephen, a friend of ours from French Harbour, physically grabbed him and shouted at him to get on the back of his motor scooter.

"They're coming after YOU!" he yelled, tugging anxiously at John's shirt. John hopped on behind him with little hesitation. Around the corner, unknown to

John, was a riot in progress. Riot, civil disturbance, revolution; we've heard various descriptions of the event over the past few days.

John could hear the gunfire, as Stephen and he sped back towards French Harbour.

"Just go home, man," ordered Stephen.

"When this happens, everybody stays home. Don't go to the bank or the store. Just go home."

"By the time he dropped me off, French Harbour was a ghost town," John told me.

"Most stores were closed, locked, and gated. The new Eldon's was open. Normally the guards carry rifles, but today the clerks had them as well. There were hardly any taxis on the road. The few that I did see, heading east towards Oak Ridge, had even more passengers packed into them than usual. Finally, I got a taxi, at a cost of 100 *lempiras* vs the usual 40 *lempira* fare because an armed guard rode in the front."

John hadn't eaten. He hadn't even made it to the bank machine for cash. To make matters worse, he was stuck sharing the taxi ride home with two girls, who ate their Bojangles chicken on the way home. The smell was torture to a hungry man.

The taxi driver's theory was that the riots had something to do with the supposedly duty-free port not being duty-free. There is a lack of reliable news on the island, especially for us, without television.

May 7, 2009

This morning, we called the Air Roatan office to check on a package we are expecting. According to the clerk, the riots are over. Thankful to hear that news, hubby headed back down island. It is a long trip and not one that he cares to take two days in a row, but we need cash.

The bank machine at the Jackson Plaza was out of service so John continued west to Coxen Hole where there are several banks. He stopped at a little restaurant/bar and watched television for a while, not understanding all the Spanish but getting the gist of it.

On the taxi ride down the island, he passed the Zolitur office, which was destroyed. Apparently, all the computers were smashed. Rumour has it that three or four rioters were shot by police, but we do not know for sure. The monthly news magazine, *The Voice,* will cover the incident when it hits the newsstands, but until then there is an information vacuum.

From the taxi window, John saw a group of 30 or 40 protesters on one side of the road. On the other side of the road, were about 30 riot police, backed up by military personnel.

The taxi floored it through the area. By the time John returned, the protesters were gone. The riot police remained. There was a group at each end of Los Fuertes and a group at RECO (that's Roatan Electric Company), which was the target of some of the protests last fall.

The unrest could spell financial suicide for the people on this island, who are already suffering from hard economic times. There was a construction boom underway until the recent recession. Hundreds of Spaniards from the mainland were brought over to work on the new cruise ship docks and numerous new resorts, condos, and other developments on the island. Most of the projects ground to a halt due to the recession, leaving workers unemployed and without the means to return to the mainland. This resulted in several incidents of civil disturbance.

The cruise ship companies threatened to remove Roatan from their itinerary if there was even one more incident. Yesterday, when the riot occurred, one regularly scheduled ship turned away. Three cruise ships that had been rerouted from Mexico, due to the Swine flu outbreak in that country, also decided not to stop in Roatan.

The airport was closed, and the ferry did not make the daily run from the mainland. Friends of ours visited West End and West Bay on Friday and the beach at West Bay was deserted. They only saw about ten tourists, compared to the hundreds you would normally count.

We went to Hole in the Wall yesterday. Two Sundays ago, the place was packed and the line for the buffet wove around the entire restaurant. Yesterday there were no tourists, only a few locals, and boaters, most of whom can't afford the $25.00, all-you-can-eat buffet.

May 22, 2009

The unrest of a couple of weeks ago seems like a distant memory, as life returns to normal here in paradise. The cruise ships have returned, and the islanders are thrilled to be back in business.

We had a conversation with Dilbert, the taxi driver who drove us from the Galaxy Breeze ferry terminal back to Oak Ridge yesterday. We caught his taxi from Oak Ridge in the morning. He offered to pick us up at 6:00 pm when the ferry returned from the mainland. True to his word, there he was, standing among all the people waiting for family and friends, easily picking us out of the crowd, and leading us to his taxi.

I asked how his day had been. He told us that he made $90.00 taking cruise ship passengers on an island tour. With an average day's salary being 200 lempiras or $10.00, that is a good day. He was looking forward to the next day when a large ship, holding 5,000 passengers, was due in. Yes, he told us, he was very happy that the cruise ships were back.

Our 50-mile trip to La Ceiba, the third-largest city in Honduras, was an unplanned, yet interesting trip and a reminder of how efficient and inexpensive the medical system in Honduras is.

Upon returning home from Hole in the Wall, Sunday evening, I had suffered what John refers to as a *Mel moment*.

"What do you want to do now?" I asked, as the captain stretched out on the settee, his novel splayed open across his chest.

"What do you mean? What's there to do?" he asked.

"It's so boring here!" I wailed, as Bob's rum punch coursed through my veins.

"It's only five o'clock, and this town is closed down. If we were down in West End, there would be a million things to do. I hate it here. When are we going to leave this boring town?"

To fight or to flee were his choices. He chose to flee, tossing his book down on the settee, and grumbling as he climbed out of the boat.

"Don't walk away on me!" I yelled as I ran after him. My foot caught the propane hose that runs across the galley floor and down I went, like a sack of potatoes, on to the steps leading up to the cabin. Luckily, they are carpeted, but it didn't do much to soften the blow as my face hit the steps.

My glasses broke, and a sharp piece of metal dug into my nose. One eye hit the step, hard. John hid behind some bushes until I gave up the search and flopped down on our bed.

Feeling like a fool, I finally walked into town on Tuesday to see Doctora Leslie, our resident doctor, about my eye.

"I'd like to make an appointment," I said sheepishly.

"Why?" she asked, smiling.

She was a middle-aged woman, of average height, with classic Latin good looks. Her black hair was worn pulled back. She was well dressed, and well-groomed, with eyeglasses hanging from her neck on a chain.

"I fell on my boat and banged my eye. I am worried that I damaged it because I am seeing fuzzy little spots."

"But why do you want to make an appointment?" she asked.

"To have you look at my eye," I answered.

"Well, come on back now," she said, turning and opening a door from the pharmacy to her office and examination room. I realized that here, unlike in Canada, appointments are not necessary.

The *doctora* tested my eye and referred me to an ophthalmologist in La Ceiba. The charge for the exam and referral was 200 lempiras, or about $10.00. There are very few specialists on the island, so patients must travel to the mainland when necessary. Regardless of the reason for our impromptu trip, I was giddy with excitement.

We had to be in Oak Ridge by 6:00 am, we figured, to reach the ferry in Dixon Cove, just this side of Coxen

Hole, in time for the 7:00 am departure. We had hoped to catch a water taxi from our dock, so we didn't have to leave our dinghy unattended in town all day. There is a constant stream of water taxis passing by our dock when we don't need one. However, we stood and stood and finally had to break down and squeeze the 15-minute walk to town into our schedule. Luckily, Dilbert saved the day, zipping us down the island in his taxi.

We raced across the Gulf of Honduras on the *Galaxy Wave*, the ferry that operates between the island and the port city of La Ceiba. The city is on the north coast of Honduras, on the southern edge of the Caribbean Sea.

Operated by Safe Way Maritime Transportation, the yacht, as the locals refer to her, is a 152-foot catamaran with four 1,825 horsepower engines with jet propulsion. She can carry 460 passengers, as well as cargo. In about an hour and fifteen minutes, we coasted into the harbor of La Ceiba under hazy skies.

A ring of jungle circled the harbor in the foreground. Beyond the rich greenery, ran a low range of mountains, grey-green in the mist. Behind that, another, much higher range, marched off to the east. A third range, highest of them all, climbed up, towards the west. Its peaks disappeared into the dark clouds.

La Ceiba reminded me of Morales in Guatemala, only larger and more modern. That is probably because the early growth of both towns back in the 1870s was due to the arrival of The Standard Fruit Company, a Dole subsidiary. Ceiba is home to about 170,000 people.

Prices on the mainland are much lower than on the island. A taxi ride anywhere within the city costs 20 lempiras or $1.00. A beer that is 40 lempiras in West End is 13 lempiras in La Ceiba. I bought three large mangoes for 25 lempiras, about the price of one mango here on the island.

Using our best Spanish, we hailed a taxi from the ferry terminal and directed the driver to take us to the *Hospital Oftamologico Ponce.* The long, straight road leading from the ferry terminal led us through an industrial area, and a less than picturesque neighborhood. Upon entering the city proper, we got our first taste of Ceiba traffic, as the driver zig-zagged like a madman through lanes of traffic, up and down streets, and through busy intersections.

BEEP! BEEP! BEEP! I thought the islanders loved tooting their horns. It was a virtual orchestra blaring all around us. After about ten minutes of this madness, the driver did a quick U-turn and pulled up in front of the hospital.

We met the *doctora*, an attractive Latin woman of middle age. She had been educated in the US, she told us, and then had lived in Montreal for some time, to learn English. She struck me as much more friendly and informal than the doctors I was used to.

"I fell on the boat and bumped my eye," I told Doctora Ponce. I didn't volunteer the details of my foolish behavior. After a thorough exam, she told me that my eyesight had not changed since my last exam, so my current eyeglass prescription is perfect.

The charge for the exam was 500 lempiras, or $25.00. She directed me to Medicentro, a large, modern medical complex, a few blocks away, to have an x-ray of my eye taken and return with the films, when they were ready. We passed on a second taxi ride and opted instead to walk the few blocks.

Two hours later, we paid for and received our x-ray films, which are now ours to keep. The cost for that was also 500 lempiras, or $25.00. We carried them back to Doctora Ponce. She studied them right away and told me that my eye was fine. There would be no permanent damage. I have a small floater in my eye, which is what is causing my fuzzy vision. It would probably disappear eventually. She said that floaters are a common occurrence with age.

La Ceiba, like a lot of Central American cities, was a little raunchy. We had been warned, of course, to be careful. However, I found the people in the city to be welcoming and friendly, as we wandered up and down the streets and through the little stalls that line them.

Hundreds, perhaps thousands of these little stalls line the roadways, built a few feet from the storefronts, with stalls and sidewalks alike covered in tarps and pieces of cloth of every color. The sidewalk becomes a shaded little tunnel that you stroll through, browsing through the largest assortment of stuff you can imagine. The storefronts are open on one side. The little stalls are piled high with wares on the other side. Chicken feed, produce, ball caps, cell phones, bras, CDs and DVDs, and pots and pans. You name it. It's there. There are more shoes than I've ever seen. I didn't think there were enough people in all of Honduras to wear all those shoes.

Many people greeted us in English, which surprised me. La Ceiba is known as the entertainment capital of Honduras and apparently, at night it gets steamy. We didn't' stay to find out. On the third Saturday in May, the *"Gran Carnaval Internacional de La Ceiba"* is held. This annual event brings 500,000 tourists to the city of 170,000 residents. The buildings along the street still wore their decorations. The carnival, I realized, had only been held five days ago.

"John, just think. If we had come here a few days ago, we could have caught the festival. Wouldn't that have been fun?" I said as I looked up at the masks hanging from the building across from us.

"AH, I don't think so, dear," said hubby.

Within 48 hours from the time I'd seen Doctora Leslie, in our town of Oak Ridge, we were back on the ferry after a positive diagnosis and an entertaining day spent in La Ceiba. The ferry left La Ceiba at 4:30 pm and arrived in Roatan just before 6:00 pm.

"Where can I land you?" asked Dilbert as he drove into Oak Ridge. Usually, the taxis drop us in town and we have a 15-minute walk, but he took us down a little back road and almost all the way to the point, saving us about ten minutes. Our legs ached after a day of constant walking, and we did what we always do when we arrive home - SHOWER!

The summer heat is upon us, and the wind has died down. Today, I showered five times. As we move from room to room, we cart our fans along with us. The afternoon heat means siesta time. The town is empty of people, as they snooze in front of fans.

May 29, 2009

I was awakened from my sleep last night by an unusual movement of the boat, like nothing I had ever felt before. She seemed to move up and down, rather than the typical side to side bump and grind. Then I heard a loud BOOM, like an explosion, and then the power went out.

I rose from my bed and peered out into the darkness, wondering if a large generator or something had blown up. The thought of an earthquake zipped through my mind in a flash, but I discarded the thought and climbed back into bed beside the captain, who, unlike me, had not stirred in the slightest.

When he stepped off the boat the next morning, John noticed that the locked door to the house was wide open. A window in the shed, which had also been locked, was open. He called the dogs and neither one came, so he checked the boathouse, where Chiquita sleeps. She wasn't there. A pile of wood lay on the ground, knocked down from the rafters where it is stored. Our 15-horsepower engine that he had been working on was in the water. Right away he suspected foul play and came to get me. We checked the house and noticed a few cups and vases knocked over and a front shutter open, but nothing else was amiss.

We unlocked the bunkhouse, where Papa John lives when he is at the Point, and discovered a horrible mess inside. Items were tossed all over. The fridge door hung wide open. A sticky mural of ketchup and syrup was splattered on the walls.

It appeared to be a case of vandalism, yet there was no sign of forced entry. All the doors and windows were locked tight. There was still no sign of the dogs. After calling them for a while, Chiquita finally came. It took longer to locate Jip, who we finally found hiding in the mangroves on the far side of the property.

I called Roatan Joe and told him the shocking news. Someone had broken into the bunkhouse during the night and made a terrible mess. I couldn't understand why the dogs hadn't barked and why they had been hiding on the far side of the property.

No sooner than I got off the phone with Roatan Joe, my friend Jeanie, from Guatemala, called.

"Did you feel the earthquake last night?" she asked me.

The memory of the odd sensation, and the bang in the night came back to me. Immediately, it all made sense. I called Roatan Joe for a second time.

"I have some good news and some bad news," I said. "We weren't broken into last night after all. That is the good news. It was only an earthquake. That is the bad news."

The power was back on by 10:00 am this morning, only seven hours after the earthquake or *terremoto*.

John zipped across the canal to Hessie's store and bought a phone card for our modem, so we had internet. The store looked even worse than the bunkhouse, with jars broken and spilled everywhere, he told me when he returned. Everywhere except the liquor shelves, which had been reinforced with an extra strip of wood. Unlike the rest of the store, there was no damage and not a drop of alcohol spilled.

We noticed water leaking through the boathouse wall and discovered a pipe broken inside the bunkhouse, no doubt caused by something falling on it. John rummaged around for a few odds and ends and repaired it in no time. While we cleaned up, we could hear our neighbors dropping broken glass into the garbage. It was much the same all over the island.

Many islanders had tuned in to their battery-operated radios during the night, heard a tsunami warning, and headed for high ground. We were told that in West End, none of the staff showed up for work at the hotels, restaurants, or stores. Resort guests were left to fend for themselves.

The scheduled cruise ship landed with no problem, which was a relief to everyone. Damage to the cruise ship dock would have spelled economic disaster. Thankfully, we have not heard of any loss of life from the earthquake.

Our list of boat jobs is endless. The most recent task is the repair and reinforcement of the stitching on the canvas on our flybridge. Almost all the pieces needed work done on them. We disassembled and piled them in a heap in our dinghy.

Our friends, Kay and Bob, live on their sailing vessel, *Bettie.* We first met them at Mario's Marina in the Rio Dulce, where we shared a hurricane season. As we spent those months together, and I got to know them, I realized that they were a very interesting couple. Bob was over six feet tall, lean, with broad shoulders and incredibly long limbs. His greying hair was clipped short and beginning to thin on the back of his head. I rarely saw him wearing shoes. Unless he was down in the Cayuco Club, he was normally bare-chested as well. He had built *Bettie* himself, which was the first thing that impressed me. He was a filmmaker, which was the second. One evening, down at the Cayuco Club, Bob presented a movie he had made of their boat travels to all the gang. I was stunned by the quality of his film and instantly inspired to work on my own home videos.

Bob towered over Kay, who was much shorter, when they stood side by side, giving them an odd couple appearance. Her brownish-grey hair was clipped close, spiking out from her head. She was as tanned as Bob. She did canvas and sewing work for some of the boaters in the Rio. We had hired her that year, at Mario's, to make us a sunscreen for our front window.

Now, *Bettie* is docked at Woodside Marina, Larry Wood's place, in Jonesville. Once again, we hired Kay, this time to resew all the stitching on our canvas. We collected it a couple of days later, for the low price of $47.00.

Picking out the miles of hand stitching I had put in over the years and cleaning all the pieces took me longer than it did for Kay to resew it. While our bedding was in the washer and then drying on the clothesline, I spread the canvas out, one piece at a time, on our bed, and worked with the wind blowing through the hatch to cool me, safe from the burning heat of the sun outside. Back up it went, piece by piece, like a puzzle, and one more job was struck from the list.

John pulled the port side transmission out of *Diamond Lil*, not an easy task as he squeezed into pretzel type positions to get at all the bolts. The dilemma was whether to repair or replace it. We took the gear assembly into Los Fuertes to have the bearing pressed off. However, the bearing was broken in the process and they had to grind it off.

Mr. Larry, who is a retired Canadian diesel mechanic, offered to help John with this repair. Together, they ground off another race, so they could get to the back-clutch pack and thrust washer.

John wrote to a Bayliner Owners Club member, who had the specs for the thrust washer and friction disks. Then he returned to Larry's shop, to measure our parts. The thrust washer cannot be repaired but the clutch pack is good, which is a relief. We have sourced the bearing in Frenh Harbour. John ordered the thrust washer and race from Florida. We cannot move the boat until the transmission is repaired and re-installed.

The motor mount on the 15-horsepower outboard motor broke, once again. A friend of ours once wisely told us that the outboard motor is the Achilles heel of cruisers. I believe him.

John and Mr. Larry began another hunt for a new mount. Off they went, in search of this old geezer and that old feller and happened to stop in at the numerous haunts that Mr. Larry frequents. Now we have several of these old islanders helping to look for the mount.

Meanwhile, in case they come up empty-handed, John believes that since he repaired the mount while we were in Guatemala and it lasted for eight months, there is nothing to lose by fixing it, once again. I sat inside the boat, writing, while he worked in his little shop, and hopefully, he has fixed it.

In the meantime, we have the 2.2-horsepower motor that Mom and Dad Wood so generously shipped to us. John mounted it on our dinghy, to get us around this Venice of the Caribbean.

Diamond Lil, docked at Oak Ridge Point

The *Galaxy Wave*, the ferry we took from Roatan to La Ceiba

Inside the *Galaxy Wave*

Pulling into the harbour in La Ceiba

Hospital *Oftalmólogo Ponce* in La Ceiba

Building on *Avenida San Isidro*, still decorated for the Carnival

John, working on the transmission

John, working on our 15-hp motor once again.

Cleaning the pieces of canvas after Kay re-stitched them

The view of Pandy Town, from the flybridge with canvas removed.

Chapter 6

June 14, 2009

Papa John, who is Roatan Joe's father, has stopped in at the Point to rest up before he sets off to take Central America by storm. Papa John is 75 years old. Despite his thick head of white hair, he appears much younger. He is tall, broad-shouldered, and still physically active and agile.

Papa John is also known around here as "Coonass John," a nickname given to him by some of his fellow ex-pats. Originally a term used to describe a person of Cajun ethnicity, in this case, I believe it is because he was originally from Louisiana.

He was never expected to live this long, after suffering a serious heart attack, years ago. Out of a group of 20 patients, he told us, he was the only one who opted not to have a heart transplant. The other 19 are dead and gone. Papa John beat the medical odds and truly appreciates each day he has on this earth.

"Life is good," we have heard him say many times, as he perches on *Diamond Lil's* step plate, his favorite spot to sit while he spins a few tales and listens to a few of ours.

"Hurry up and leave," he told us, last night, "so you can get back. Once you are return, then I can leave. Meanwhile, I need to rest for a few days before I head back to the mainland."

Resting up for Papa John meant beginning the day bright and early, with a swim and snorkel while we young folk were still yawning over our morning coffee.

Then, he set off on his four-wheeler (no golf cart for this old boy) to the early morning market to buy fresh vegetables and scout around for a young, well-muscled local kid to assist John with the heavy, awkward part of the transmission job, which is putting it back in.

Papa John returned to the Point with a polite young black man named Garwin Pandy. He looked to be in his mid-twenties and sported an impish smile that gave the impression that he found life to be constantly amusing. His smile lit up his face and radiated through his eyes. When he spoke, he referred to himself in the third person. "Garwin thinks you have beautiful plants, Miss Melanie," he said, as he passed our ever-growing collection of plants on the dock.

He had the heavy transmission hauled from the workshop and along the dock to *Diamond Lil* faster than I could turn on my camera and capture it on film.

John supervised while Superman heaved, hauled, and grunted down in the bilge. I hovered around the back deck, wiping Superman's oily fingerprints from the fiberglass around the engine room door. Unlike John likes to do, he couldn't tell me to go away!

Before long, the repaired transmission was back in place. John fired up *Diamond Lil's* engines,Many ha to test it. Back and forth, from forward to reverse, back to forward, straining the dock lines (and breaking one), but the news was good. The repair was successful.

Papa John decided that Captain John was such a good supervisor that he'd have him supervise a few jobs that he needed done in the bunkhouse. The earthquake left the bunkhouse more than a little misaligned. In return for John's assistance, Papa John paid Superman for our job as well. This teamwork is great!

Papa John is here to relieve us, so we are mobile once again. Captain John, or house-sitting John as he is known at Hole in the Wall, and I are off for a week in West End. I had to chuckle when I gave Papa John instructions on feeding his dogs and asked him to please water my plants, which are in fact his plants. Roatan Joe told us to think of the place as ours. I admit that I'm beginning to feel like it is.

June 16, 2009

If there is anything that makes one appreciate the open sea, it's a few months spent at the dock. Yes, it is second best, I admit, sometimes even the best, for the time being. But being out there, well, that's what it's all about. We had a flat calm, perfect power boating weather day for our 22-mile cruise to West End.

Out went the fishing lines because apparently, this summer heat makes the fish bite. We chugged slowly past West Bay and West End, rounded Gibson Point and fished a little bay that is supposed to be good for tuna. Then back to West End, where we picked up a mooring ball in the Marine Park that surrounds West End and

Sandy Bay. We are back to crystal clear water. Yahoo.

I feel like a tourist with only a week to soak up all the scenery and activity here. I'm not though, which is the best part. Walking through town, we meet up with people we know. As I munch on a burrito, watching the boats floating peacefully in the turquoise bay and the passersby, I tell John that this is my favorite town, anywhere!

"Three months," I reminded him. "You promised me that we would only stay at the dock for three months. We have been there for over two months already."

"It's not like we are stuck there all the time, Mel. We are free to go cruising whenever Papa John is here on the island. We came to West End as you wanted. We are heading to the Cayos Cochinos for a few days. So, quit your bitching."

June 17, 2009

The Cayos Cochinos, or Hog Islands, lie about 20 miles south of Roatan and 20 miles north of mainland Honduras. The two main islands are Cayo Grande, which is inhabited, and Cayo Menor, which is not, except by rangers and scientists from the Coral Reef Foundation Research Institute, who are stationed there.

The Cayos Cochinos consists of the two small islands and 13 small coral cays, and was declared a Marine Protected Area in 1993 by the Honduras government and then a Marine Natural Monument in 2003. No anchoring is permitted but there are mooring balls available.

The cost to moor is $10.00 per night for the boat and each crew member. The captain stays for free. Excursions to the Cayos Cochinos are popular in Roatan and Lower Monitor Cay, which is home to a Garifuna community called Chachauate, who serve up traditional fish meals, although they have no running water or electricity on the island.

We stocked up on gasoline, water, and groceries in West End, since there are no stores or supplies in the Cayos Cochinos. We were underway by about 1:00 pm. We pulled into the mooring field at Cayo Grande by about 4:00 pm. The skies opened as we arrived, so we quickly snagged a ball in front of the Plantation Beach Resort for the night.

We woke to crystal clear water and set off exploring in our dinghy. The sea was choppy, so we opted for land travel and hiked along a trail to the top of Cayo Grande. The lighthouse, which apparently offers a spectacular view of both the mainland and of Roatan, was locked, but we enjoyed the hike regardless.

We returned to the boat for some snorkeling and decided to move to a prettier location. We had spied a private little cove beside some rocks that reminded us of our own Georgian Bay, with a gorgeous reef about 20 feet away and a private little beach.

The setting was idyllic, and I painted while John snorkeled and read. We chilled and swam and relaxed and barbequed and napped. It was heavenly.

June 22, 2009

On our return trip to West End on Friday, we snagged a big Barracuda, which we mistook at first for a Wahoo. John hadn't even walked across the aft deck from one line to set the second line when the fish landed, and the wrestling began. We put him on ice in our bathtub, the usual fish locker and offered him to friends once we arrived in West End. Many hands make light work, and he was cleaned in a flash and shared among neighbors. We came home with a serving for two, which is all we need.

After an enjoyable getaway, we headed back to the dock at the Point. Calm West End seas lured us into thinking that it would be a smooth ride. Once we cleared the West Bay banks and veered east, Mother Ocean had other plans. We were once again bounced and banged and soaked and tossed about, but in three short hours, we were home, tied up with the power cord plugged in.

Hoisting the dinghy from its mount on our stern, we threw on the outboard motor and off we went to Hole in the Wall to hear a friend from West End play his guitar. But alas, he had left just before we arrived, after entertaining the crowd for several hours.

Today, I washed and hung laundry and did some writing in the boat. John shopped and puttered around the yard and sat in his captain's chair, on our 'Gone with the Wind' style verandah, gazing out to sea with a cold glass of lemonade and a good book in his hand.

Diamond Lil enjoyed a bath after her saltwater shower yesterday and is tucked in all squeaky clean for the night in her little berth. Our doggies have resumed their position on the dock outside our back door for the ritual after dinner, after dishes, bedtime doggie snacks.

Papa John left for the mainland this afternoon, from here by four-wheeler to his truck in Oak Ridge, and then down to the ferry terminal near Coxen Hole, where he will park the truck until he returns. He will travel by ferry to La Ceiba, where he shares an apartment with a friend and after that, only time will tell.

"Not much time left," he told us one evening as he sat chatting on the side of *Diamond Lil*, "And still a lot of traveling I want to do. I'm a gypsy, you know. I always have been."

Yeah, we know Papa John, we know. We're gypsies too.

July 14, 2009

We have been in the news again due to the supposed "coup", the marching of Honduras' President, Mel Zelaya, out of his bedroom in his pajamas and swift exodus to Costa Rica in the dark of the night.

"How many Presidents do we have today?" was the ice breaker at the July 4th party we attended a couple of weeks ago at our neighbor and long-time resident Miss

Sandy Byrd's place, on the Point. We were a mixture of gringos, most of whom are now residents of Honduras, and locals, seating ourselves on Miss Sandy's spacious verandah overlooking the sea, making shy introductions.

Tall, white pillars made me feel like I was back in New Orleans, where Miss Sandy comes from. Her place is a lush, green oasis, dropped into the middle of the otherwise rocky, sandy spit of land.

We met Miss Sandy and Miss Donna on the first night we spent at the dock on The Point. Since then, we met another neighbor, Miss Jessie, or Aunt Jessie, as most people call her.

Jessie Cooper is a lively octogenarian, who has lived much of her life in her little white wooden house on the Point. She is a white islander, of medium height, with curly grey hair and brown eyes. She is as agile as most people half her age, I think to myself, as I watch Alana walk her Mom along the narrow concrete sidewalk that winds along the sea and through the mangroves, from her house to Miss Sandy's. Arm in arm they climbed the broad steps to the verandah, chattering back and forth in their thick island brogue.

We first met Alana when she came to the Point to remove Jip's stitches. She is a petite woman in her 50's, with a friendly manner and big smile. She pulled up a chair next to me and began chatting with another woman whom I could tell was a close friend. We were introduced to Lori Soule, and her husband, Mark Thiem, for the first time. Alana and Lori were reminiscing about a girls' party they had held to celebrate Lori's birthday the week before. I silently wished I had met them sooner since I spent most of my time socializing with the man-crowd around Jonesville. A girl's party sounded like great fun.

Lori, like Alana, was a slight woman. Her shorts and tank top revealed long, muscular limbs. She wore her long, dark brown hair pulled back in a ponytail. Bangs hung over her green eyes, which were framed by thick, black lashes. Lori's deep and distinctive voice was the first thing that struck me about her. Her laugh was loud and contagious.

Her husband, Mark, was squirming in his chair and groaning in discomfort. He was tall, broad-shouldered, with neatly trimmed brown hair and brown eyes. He had fallen off a ladder a few days ago while working on their house, he told us. They had purchased a waterfront lot in nearby Calabash Bight and were building their own home. After a short visit, he begged forgiveness and headed for home to try to get more comfortable.

Lori and Alana asked Miss Sandy if they could borrow a cooler for their beer. They were going to have a sleepover at Alana's house after the party. It sounded like fun. Again, I felt a stab of envy.

A few days ago, we woke to find white flags, bedsheets, anything white, flying from homes and boats onshore. I asked Miss Sandy what was up when I called to discuss what we should bring to the party.

"The white flags show support for the new government," she told me. Someone, I am not sure quite who, came around and asked her to fly a white flag or put out something white to show support for Micheletti, so she hauled out a big sheet and laid it on her lawn.

We have yet to meet a Honduran who wants Zelaya back. There is a huge relief that he is gone. We receive little or no news but hear many rumors. One rumor was that Zelaya was planning to sneak into the country through Roatan. That got everyone excited for a while and apparently the airport was closed.

There is a dusk to dawn curfew in effect in the country, but you would never know it here. The nightlife continues unimpeded. Religious groups meet and sing and pray ALL night long. The cool evening air brings people out to socialize, and the "kids" get hopping around 11:00 pm. Music fills the night air, and boats whizz back and forth. Curfew? Ha! However, we did hear that in West End, the tourism center of the island, the curfew was in effect which would be a terrible blow to the tourism industry.

Last week, we were invited to a full moon party by our friend Larry Wood and his girlfriend Norma. We dinghied down to Larry's place and drove with them to the swanky gated community of Parrot Tree Plantation.

Parrot Tree sits approximately halfway between Oak Ridge and French Harbour on the south side of the island. We had seen the place from the water, as we passed in *Diamond Lil* and had seen the yellow brick entranceway from the winding road that runs down the island but had never been inside the complex. WOW.

The property is enormous and includes a marina, condos, homes, beaches, restaurants, a gorgeous pool, and short-term rental units. The place was stunning, but unfortunately quite empty. Only one woman swam in the enormous pool. She told us, alternating between Spanish and English, that she worked and lived on the property.

Most locals are bilingual, and I find it amusing the way a single conversation switches back and forth between English and Spanish. I sat in the doctor's office with a group of local women one day, waiting for my turn with Doctora Leslie. It was a few days after the earthquake. I chuckled to myself, listening to the women as they chattered away, back and forth between the two languages.

"An der he was," one woman told about her husband sleeping through the earthquake, as did John, "jusa snorin ana droolin tru da hole ting." Sometimes their English is as difficult to make out as their Spanish.

Expats take turns hosting the full moon parties, always held on the night of the full moon, regardless of which day of the week it falls on. There are many Americans residing here and judging by these homes, many have money. The house was gorgeous, overlooking the sea, with a pool up on the balcony. We met several new people, and it was interesting, but we both came away with a feeling that we had little in common with them.

We were quite content to climb back into our small but cozy home. I chuckled to think that our whole living area was smaller than the washroom in the house at Parrot Tree. As we reflected on our evening, we agreed that we are beginning to feel more comfortable socializing with the locals we have come to know than some of the wealthy gringos on the island.

Sundays are refreshingly quiet in Oak Ridge. Hessie's is the only store open and only until noon. Boat traffic is sparse, especially in the morning. Most people go to church and then spend the afternoon with their families.

We look forward to the Sunday BBQ at the McNab Place, or Puky's. Gerald McNab, nicknamed Puky, and his wife, Norma, are the Mom and Pop of the branch of the Roatan McNab family that recently opened what become one of the favorite eateries on the east end of the island.

Whether you travel by land or by sea, a matching set of white gates welcomes you to Puky's. The land entrance is located across from a convenient parking lot on the north side of the picturesque road that runs from the main island highway down into the charming fishing village of Jonesville. The seaside entrance is through a matching white set of gates at the end of a dock built on the scenic south shore of the island.

Fleets of giant shrimp and lobster boats line the shore while dories and skiffs zip back and forth along the inner channel, a protected waterway that serves as the main route of transport for residents of communities from Calabash Bight to First Bight.

On a cloudless day, the giant peaks of the mountain ranges of the Honduran mainland, about thirty miles away, form a stunning backdrop to the azure waters of the Caribbean Sea stretching to the south.

Townsfolk saunter along the narrow roadway through Jonesville, one of the oldest communities on the island, and children entertain with good old-fashioned outdoor fun that is heartwarming to watch. Here, three generations of the McNab family work and live in harmony. Before long, you begin to feel like a part of this warm and welcoming island family.

After dinner, we strolled along the narrow roadway through Jonesville to get some exercise. It is a quaint town, residents are mostly of English or Cayman ancestry, white, and well off compared to the average islander.

Lobster season opened July 1st and we learned that shrimp season may or may not open then. A few boats go out, to take samples. Then, they decide whether the season should open. Apparently, this year the opening was delayed for shrimp. There is a lot of activity, with the large fishing boats taking on crew and heading out, after months of repairs, and in many cases, flashy new paint jobs.

The processing plant in Oak Ridge has a FOR HIRE sign out, a positive development. We overhear locals discussing what will happen if the international community imposes trade sanctions. Who will buy the lobster and shrimp? Let's hope there is a market for them after all this work and money getting the fleet ready to head out. .

The captain got in on a diesel fuel purchase deal at a great price and we took on some fuel. If trouble did come to the island we could cut and run and have enough fuel to get to Guatemala. Don't worry though, Roatan Joe. We have no plans to go anywhere - it's just nice to know we could, should we have to.

August 9, 2009

Painting gives me a lot of pleasure. Our two-year-old grandson, Tyler, liked the photo I took of Grampa with the barracuda he caught on our way home from the Cayos Cochinos. When he saw the blood, he said "Ew mommy - big fishy crashed." I painted him a picture of John with his barracuda and one of a sea-turtle so he will know us as the boating, albeit absentee grandparents.

Currently, 13 of my original paintings are somewhere between Honduras and Ontario and I hope they arrive eventually. I shipped them with a local company called RAS or Roatan Air Services and they seem to have vanished.

It never ceases to amaze me just how many Canadian and American people live down here in the Bay Islands. We popped into Hole in the Wall one afternoon this week and met another such family, a young couple with one daughter, around 12 years of age.

They live in California for ten months of the year and down here for two months. They own property on the island and lived here full time for many years. We were all laughing and telling stories about the bizarre things that happen down here. The woman said that back at home, in California, when something strange happens, they say, "That's just so Honduran."

I had a very "Honduran" experience while shopping in Coxen Hole, recently. I stopped in at my favorite little lunch spot and was paying for my shrimp, mashed potatoes, and vegetables when I spied a single bottle of Lipton Iced Tea in the refrigerator.

I had walked a long way in the heat and was parched, so I quickly snatched up the last cold iced tea from the fridge, paid for my meal, and sat down at the table closest to the cash register. I opened the bottle and took a long, thirsty haul from it.

"YUCK," I blurted out loud.

"That is the WORST iced tea I've ever tasted. I think it has gone bad," I said to the girl at the cash register.

"That's not iced tea," she replied, "That's why I didn't charge you for it."

"What is it?" I asked, wondering if I had just swallowed some type of cleanser, which is what it tasted like.

"It's her medicine," she said, pointing back towards the kitchen and laughing so hard her belly shook. By now everyone in the restaurant was listening to the exchange, chuckling, but not shocked because it is just so typically 'Honduran.'

"It won't hurt you," she assured me "And I DIDN'T charge you for it." That was her main concern through the entire exchange.

"Well, could you PLEASE go back and ask her just what it is?" I asked pleasantly, "Or send her out."

She sauntered back into the kitchen and returned, a few minutes later. "It will make you feel good," she said, "It's to purge you."

"It's not going to purge me on my long taxi ride home or anything is it?" I asked, having visions of yelling "BAJA" halfway home and having a carload of people wait while I dashed into the jungle to be "purged."

"Oh no dear, nothing like that," she chuckled, as did the rest of the patrons.

"Would you like anything else to drink? The tamarind juice is very good," she said.

I sat back down with my cold tamarind juice and continued eating my fresh shrimp. A minute later I looked up as a blonde woman, whom I assumed was from the visiting cruise ship, because blondes are few and far between here, reached into the fridge and snatched up the very same bottle of iced tea.

"I wouldn't drink that if I was you," I said to the woman. "It's not iced tea. It's somebody's medicine."

She thanked me and returned the bottle to the fridge without so much as batting an eye. She explained that she used to live here, and was not surprised when something 'Honduran' happened.

Papa John, chatting with us on the back deck of *Diamond Lil*

Miss Sandy's house on Oak Ridge Point, as seen from the sea

Don Cameron (left) and Larry Wood (right), filling DL with diesel.

Woodside Marina in Blue Rock, Roatan

The Full Moon Party at Parrot Tree Plantation

Full Moon Party at Parrot Tree Plantation

The roadside entrance to McNab Place, or, Puky's, in Jonesville.

My painting of Captain John, with the big fishy that crashed.

Chapter 7

September 1, 2009

The three months that we planned to spend tied to the dock at Oak Ridge Point has now been five months. However, we still have repairs to complete, which are so much easier done on land, claims hubby. At times, I feel content here onshore. Other times, I long to be back at sea. Since we are here, we decided to tackle the next boat project on our list, the HEAD! Not the actual toilet, but the bathroom.

I firmly believe that the shower in *Diamond Lil* has had more use than any shower on any Bayliner on the planet. Living in this hot, sticky climate means sometimes taking three, four, or even five showers in a single day. It's the only way to cool off, other than a swim, which also needs to be followed by a freshwater shower.

The sailboat people are saying, "Cry me a river," because our shower must seem decadent to them as they stand bare ass on deck under their plastic bags full of water. But after four years on this ship, I can't imagine living without it. Well, except for now, of course. Roatan Joe has offered to let us use the shower in the house for the few days it will take for our bathroom renovations.

I peeled the wallpaper off the walls, and John removed the wood from both sides of the shower. He bought some plywood from the building supply place in town and hauled it home in the dinghy. The piece of wood was almost as big as the dinghy, but he got it here. First, he rebuilt the wall between the shower and our cabin (bedroom) and coated it with fiberglass.

We compared prices of various colors of Formica for the inside of the shower and ended up with a glossy white one which was available right here in Oak Ridge at a lower price than the main building supply places down-island. We always try to support the local economy when possible.

The first piece of Formica was cut, measured, and installed with no problem. The next piece was larger, with many odd angles that needed to be cut. I watched John measure and mark, re-measure, and check. "Measure twice, cut once, he always told me."

I watched him climb in and out of *Diamond Lil* several times, clutching the piece he was cutting to the perfect shape. I watched him squeeze carefully through the door into the head and then squeeze back out, hauling the huge piece of Formica.

Finally, all the cuts were perfect, and the edges were ground down with our Dremel tool. The glue went on the wooden wall and then on the back of the Formica. We carefully attempted to position it, but before it was in place, the glue stuck like, well glue! We quickly tried to pull the Formica back off the wall and we heard, "CRACK!" Of course, it was me that pulled too hard and a huge, long crack appeared down the center of the piece.

It's great to be a girl because tears just happen so easily at a time like this. I am sure that John wanted to cry also but he was too upset to even utter his favorite swear word.

A couple of days later, the replacement piece was ever so carefully measured, re-measured, and cut. Once again, the glue went on both the wall and the back of the Formica. We had a plan this time, and had moved some obstructions to make it an easier fit. We edged it into place, ever so slowly. It touched the wall in just one tiny spot. John tried to pull it, and I said, "OH NO. The same thing is happening again."

He didn't have a chance to even complete the word "NO," when we heard a loud CRACK. We broke the second piece, just like the first.

I am beginning to question the strength of this Formica when I picture *Diamond Lil* crashing and banging in the big waves out there. I have visions of crawling down to use the head and finding it in pieces. The captain insists that it will work.

My camera is the latest victim of salt air and is no longer functioning so, unfortunately, the pictures of the head job stopped just before the Formica went on. Perhaps it is just as well. Our matching pieces of cracked Formica, the chaotic scene in the boat with missing walls, and trim and tools everywhere, wouldn't make a very pretty picture.

The captain surfed the internet and found a similar camera for sale. We ordered it online, and shipped it to Roatan Joe's house in Rockford, Illinois. He is flying

down on September 12th and has offered to bring it to
the island for me.

September 28, 2009

A three-hour cruise with the wind to our back and a
gentle following sea had us in West End, the tourist
trap of the island, *sans* tourists. We were alone in the
mooring field when we first arrived. Eventually, one
other boat, a sailboat, with the typical herding instinct
we notice all too often, proceeded to snag the closest
mooring ball to us, although there were a dozen more
private spots from which to choose. It's not as easy to
fulfill the deserted, devil may care, no modesty-required
anchorage down here in the Caribbean as you might
imagine.

Suffering from the decline in tourism due to the political
crisis on the mainland, West End was ready for a party
when we arrived. The annual fishing tournament and
festival were underway. Hundreds of people were
pouring into town. Tourists were few and far between,
however. Instead, the crowds of people arriving for the
occasion were locals.

Colorful little booths, decorated with party beads and
palm fronds, lined a long stretch of the white sandy road
that is West End. Island fare was served up - jerk
chicken, lasagna, curry meatballs, ribs, pork, chicken,
chicken, and more chicken. Red beans, rice, coleslaw,
and tortillas - no meal would be complete without them.
Oh, and *tajadas*, pieces of deep-fried plantain, which the
captain has developed a taste for. Cholesterol count, you

must be joking, this is Central America. Deep fry it, and hopefully, it won't make you sick.

Extended families poured out of buses, vans, taxis, SUVs, and water taxis. Many lugged huge pots of already prepared meals, *frescos* (pop), and adult libations. After parking in the shade along the beach, they ate, drank, and watched the kids swim and play.

In addition to the few local boats and water taxis in the harbor, several fishing trawlers and yachts lined the docks. Occasionally, another yacht would arrive, but without fish. Then, a small dory pulled right up on the beach. Crowds of people flocked to the boat, surrounding it on all sides. Much display was made of hauling the huge marlin out and carrying him to stage central to be measured, weighed, and photographed.

I don't mind crowds, so while John sat on the party barge watching from a safe distance, I dug my way deep into the throng swarming the monstrous fish to take photos. The crowd carried me forward until I was close enough to get a shot, well, sort of. The Honduran idea of closeness is much closer than what we are used to. However, I'll do a lot for a good shot.

The awards ceremony was so long that I was afraid we would miss it when we dashed out to the boat to shower and change, a necessity in these climes. However, upon returning, we found the awards ceremony still well underway. Nothing goes quickly here.

Three different disc jockeys played three different kinds

of music along the street. There was one with a real Latin influence, one with more of a reggae beat, and a third that we didn't stop to listen to. There was also a local gringo band with people we see all the time here, in town, so we watched them for a while. We ended up dancing in the street to the reggae tunes.

We stayed out way too late and took a few quiet days to recover. During this time, we discovered a huge hole in the dinghy, and we had to drag it to shore. No dinghy means no means of travel between shore and *Diamond Lil* on her mooring ball.

Luckily, our friends, Lonny and Cynthia, invited us to tie up to their dock, haul the dinghy up on their gorgeous West End white sandy beachfront for repair, and just hang out. So, we spent the last six days on what I feel is the prettiest part of West End - right beside Ronnie's Barefoot Beach bar where we enjoyed our Christmas dinner last year.

The party barge, built and opened by a fellow Canadian, Captain Perry, from Niagara Falls, pulled up on the beach beside *Diamond Lil,* and we had ourselves a happening little stretch of sand. That was until Cowboy Mel Zelaya showed up in his white hat, and ruined all the fun.

Actually, curfew, or the touch as it is referred to in our translated Spanish news, was kind of fun, well for me, being of strange mind. It reminded me of a good old Canadian holiday, a quiet day, with stores closed. It was a pleasant change. Everyone stayed home. Police drove down the road waiting at each shop to see it closed and the people heading home. Traffic could leave town but not enter. As *touristas* or gringos, we appear to be invisible. We walk anywhere we like, to the store and back, and nobody bats an eye. We stocked up on cash, always the first thing to go when trouble looms, and a few necessities. The rum shelves were empty. People wondered if the cigarette supply would last.

Lonny brought in a huge marlin himself just days after the tournament. The beast weighed almost 300 pounds, and we watched it being cleaned. Wow, what a lot of meat. Cynthia says it's the same every year, either right before or right after the tournament, they get a big one, but never at the tournament. He also brought in about six tunas, and gave us two. John stuffed one with his homemade salsa and grilled it. It was delicious!

Earlier in the week, our new friends, Mark and Lori from Calabash Bight, came down to spend an afternoon with us. I really enjoyed their visit. We had lunch at Sundowners, a drink at Ronnie's, and sat on Lonny's beachfront property under his palapa doing nothing as people do here. We went out to the boat to swim, and then back to town. We were thankful for Lonny's son Anthony. He ferried us around in his water taxi because our dinghy was lying on its side in the sand while the glue dried.

Our week in West End was just what I needed. I walked the stretch a hundred times, and savored it each time. Perry and I chatted one afternoon as we sat aboard the *Reef Rider* about just what makes West End so special. I can't tell you, you'd have to come to see and even then, you wouldn't see, unless you stayed a while. On the last day, people said, "You're leaving." How do they know?

We bade our hosts farewell and enjoyed an equally pleasant cruise home, catching a rare south breeze that made the sea lie down for us. It was nice to be back.

We had a day or two here, at the Point, before Joe headed home after his working holiday. Papa John flew back to the States for his flu shot and doctors' appointments, once the airlines reopened after the alleged departure of Honduran President Mel Zelaya. He will return to the island in November.

Replacing the walls around the shower in our head.

John, returning from Oak Ridge, with our plywood.

New friends, Mark and Lori, under Lonny's palapa in West End.

Lobster and crab – grilled on the boat.

The roadside bar at the West End Fishing Tournament

DL on the dock in West End – with Lonny's marlin.

Chapter 8

October 14, 2009

"I think it's time for the book, Mel," wrote Mel. No, that's not a typo.

John and I first met Mel and his wife Cathy at the Lockport lock, where the Chicago Sanitary Ship Canal meets the Des Plains River. We had just completed an exhausting, albeit exhilarating cruise from the Windy City along the Chicago River, right through downtown Chicago.

Under Lakeshore and Columbus, we had come, past the Chicago Tribune, under Michigan Ave, past the Wrigley Building, under Wabash, past Marina City where tall, cylindrical towers wrapped with balconies curled gently amid the cityscape.

We had traveled 40 miles and under 54 bridges, including two fixed bridges with a clearance of only 17 feet that had required the removal of our radar. Then, we left the city behind and wove our way through an obstacle course of monstrous barges, some moving, and others docked along the side of the canal.

I scrambled out onto the high, rough, but free concrete wall to secure *Diamond Lil*, for the night. Directly behind us along the wall in their little sailing vessel *Starsinger*, were Cathy and Mel.

Their heads popped up from down below in their boat as I sat nursing scraped knees from my scramble up the rough wall. They looked to be, like us, forty-something.

Mel had thick, straight, prematurely white hair and a white mustache and goatee. Sparkly blue eyes smiled from behind his square, wire-rimmed glasses, and his pink cheeks rounded with amusement as he spoke with an ever so slight lisp. Cathy wore her reddish-blonde hair cut short and was a little quieter and more reserved than her captain.

Drawn by each other's Canadian flags, we exchanged pleasantries as boaters often do. They had come from Sioux Lookout, in northern Ontario. We had left our hometown of Keswick on Lake Simcoe, Ontario, along the Trent Severn Waterway to Georgian Bay, west along the North Channel to Lake Huron, through the Mackinac Straits to Lake Michigan, south along the eastern shore of Michigan and across the big old lake to Chicago.

We were headed south as were virtually all the cruisers that we met along the way. Some were cruising the Great Circle Loop. Others were headed for Florida and many of them, like us, were headed for the Bahamas Islands or the Caribbean.

We waved to each other once again the next morning as we waited for the lock to open, yet unaware of a lasting friendship being born. Later that day, as we pulled up to the wall in Joliet, Illinois, *Starsinger* was casting off, and we chuckled and waved for the second time that day.

The following day, as we were entering the Dresden lock on the Illinois River with a group of RVs, or Recreational Vehicles as the lockmasters along the inland waterway refer to pleasure boats, we once again spotted *Starsinger*. In fact, we recognized each of the vessels that were about to lock through with us. We had all been funneled from the wide waters of the Great Lakes into the narrows of the Inland Waterway.

In front of us were Lew and Virgil on *Vagabond*, a 42' Grand Banks. John and I had met Lew and his wife Karen the previous year in the boater friendly town of Elizabeth City, North Carolina so we were surprised to spot the boat again. Lew had just sold the boat to Virgil and was traveling with him for a few days to show him the ropes. This we had discovered when we joined them aboard their vessel for a cold beer back in Joliet.

Ahead of *Vagabond* were Cathy and Mel on *Starsinger*. Ahead of *Starsinger* was *Christine Marie* with Mary and Dennis on board. Dennis and Mary had stopped alongside *Lil Diamond* at the wall in Munroe Harbour in downtown Chicago to introduce themselves to us during the week we spent there. We had developed a quick friendship. Ahead of *Christine Marie*, in the lead heading into the lock was *Sea Fox*, a 49' Kroegen that we had anchored beside in the Benjamin Islands in the North Channel a couple of weeks earlier.

Because the RVs or pleasure boats are usually locked through together as a group separately from the tows and barges, it is not uncommon to travel together. As luck would have it, we all met up again downriver at the Marseilles lock. The lockmaster had just informed us, on his VHF radio, that we would have a bit of a wait before locking through. Most of the group elected to drop anchor. but John decided to stay up on the flybridge with the engines idling while I ducked downstairs to make lunch.

The VHF radio downstairs crackled to life as I worked away in the galley. Milt, from *Sea Fox*, was asking if anyone in the group was interested in buying a used Follow Me Satellite TV system. Between lunch and locking through, I found myself carefully passing a cash deposit and boat card in a plastic bag on the end of our longest boat hook over to Fran, Milt's wife on *Sea Fox*, and planning to meet up downriver to pick up our new dish.

It was an eventful lock through, as *Starsinger*, the second vessel to enter the lock, stalled and had trouble restarting. Mary and Dennis came to the rescue and towed her out of the lock. Mel finally got the engine started, and the boat continued under her own power briefly before stalling again.

Tents lined the river for miles on end. Liquored-up vacationers on wave runners and in small powerboats shot up and down the river. We hooked up a stern line, and towed *Starsinger*. John and Mel discussed the possible causes of the engine trouble on the radio, as I filmed the chaotic scene in the water around us.

Mary and Dennis, on *Christine Marie*, went on ahead to find dockage for all of us in Ottawa, Illinois. Over the VHF radio, John admitted to being a "retired mechanic." Mary quickly came back to say that there is no such thing as a "retired" mechanic.

So, there on the banks of the Illinois River, in the small town of Ottawa, the friendship began to grow. John helped Mel with the engine repairs while Mary, Cathy, and I ventured into town to find the laundromat and grocery store.

Mary called me over to where she was sitting, while she waited for her clothes to dry. She showed me the travel website, on her laptop, that she was using to share her trip with friends and family back home. I was hooked! Before long, I had signed up for my own site.

Cathy and Mel insisted on treating all of us to a delicious dinner that evening at a Mexican restaurant to thank us for the help. We traded boating stories over cold Coronas and frosty Margaritas. The following night, we invited the gang to join us on *Diamond Lil* for some of the captain's famous jerk chicken. Once again, we shared stories and laughs with Cathy, Mel, Mary, and Dennis.

Cathy and Mel were making their trip south on *Starsinger* in multiple legs and only had a few weeks to move the boat as far south as possible on this, the first leg. Not only was their schedule tighter than ours but their little sailboat traveled more slowly than our powerboats, and we drifted apart after leaving Ottawa, Illinois.

On we went through Peoria, Beardstown, Grafton, and Alton, Illinois, and into the mighty Mississippi for a 218-mile trip to the Ohio River. North on the Ohio River, we traveled for 58 miles until we reached the

Cumberland River and the green hills of Kentucky. We entered the Barkley lock and dam, where we were raised 57 feet to Barkley Lake. Then, we traveled the short distance to Green Turtle Bay Marina, near the town of Grand Rivers, Kentucky.

It was here that we ran into Mel once again, two weeks after parting ways back in Ottawa, IL. Cathy had already flown home to return to work while Mel made arrangements to leave *Starsinger* at a nearby marina until they could get away to make the next leg of their trip south.

It was here that I discovered that Mel was a movie producer by trade, and the timing couldn't have been more perfect. My new digital movie camera was making me crazy. My memory was full, and I couldn't download my footage. Mel came to the rescue, and I made notes as he walked me through the process.

Mel flew home a few days later to join Cathy and plan the next leg of their cruise south. That was September of 2006. We continued south through Kentucky, Tennessee, Alabama, and Mississippi. I logged our progress on our website, and could always count on Mel to respond to my entries, becoming one of my most loyal readers.

I mailed him copies of my finished videos, and he always wrote back with feedback and suggestions. It meant a lot to me. We took a road trip from Mobile, Alabama to The Big Easy, New Orleans, Louisiana. When I immersed myself in the Halloween festivities on

Bourbon St., and lost my expensive digital video camera, Mel wrote, "Mel, I think it's time for the book."

From the moment John and I walked up the six grey steps to the balcony in front of the house, here at Oak Ridge Point, and looked out at the breathtaking beauty, I thought to myself, if I can't write here, I can't write anywhere.

I begin my workday by sweeping the terra cotta tile floor of the great room. All the floors on the first level of the house are covered in a layer of thick, yellowed varnish. Once I peeled the first piece off and saw the drastic improvement, I couldn't stop. And so, day by day up comes the scabby looking surface.

I sweep and think and then sit down to write. When I stumble upon a writer's block, I get up and sweep and think until I can continue writing. The entire front wall of the great room consists of sliding doors and windows, which open all the way. The side of the room facing *Diamond Lil* is also made up of a large door and set of windows that open in the same fashion. The wall to my right, facing the sea, also has a window that opens fully, so the trade winds flow through the room. There are no screens, so it feels like I am writing in the great outdoors.

The commute from *Diamond Lil* takes about 30 seconds in the morning and another 30 seconds when I stroll back to break for lunch, which John makes while I work. After lunch, I wander back to my island office and write for a few more hours.

My end of the workday whistle comes in the form of the sound of our ice-maker full of freshly made ice being dumped into the cooler we keep on the back deck of *Diamond Lil.* This means that John has decided it is beer-thirty. I save my work and log the number of words I have written My goal is 1,500 words a day. I tidy my desk, weighing down the piles of paper with conch shells, close the windows and doors, and make the 30-second commute back to the boat.

October 26, 2009

The captain and I were invited to join some friends on an outing "out east." This meant traveling towards the east end of the island to visit Marble Hill Farms, a resort on the north side of the island, overlooking the ex-pat community of Punta Blanca.

Larry Wood, also known as Mr. Larry, or Senor Grumpy – my nickname for him, offered us a ride to the event. Since we have no vehicle, we jumped at the chance to explore more of the island. Mr. Larry drove up the hill from Oak Ridge and headed east, where pavement gave way to a dusty dirt road. Not far out of town, we hung a left through a matching pair of stone walls, with a Marble Hill Farms sign carved into wood.

A long, shady driveway, flanked on both sides by tall bamboo trees, led through the property to the Crow's Nest Restaurant. The open-air building was surrounded by lush tropical gardens. An upper deck provided a magnificent view of the north shore and the community of Punta Blanca off in the distance, slightly to the west.

The event turned out to be a going-away party for a woman named Joy, an ex-pat who is leaving the island to spend a few months stateside. Although I had never met Joy, she graciously invited me to her property to take cuttings from a variety of 200 different tropical plants. It appears that I am beginning to grow roots!

On the way home, Senor Grumpy pulled up beside an odd little roadside bar in Spanish Hill, the community just up the hill from Oak Ridge. The ambiance left a little to be desired, as we parked along the side of the road. What bar, I wondered at first until I realized that the little wooden shack that we were heading for was painted in the Salva Vida blue and yellow colors. Sun-faded posters decorated the weathered walls and a string of old Christmas lights hung over the door. We pulled up plastic chairs, blue to match the Salva Vida décor and set our drinks – Salva Vida, of course, on the weathered old blue bench in front of the building.

The vista was in stark contrast to the one we had been treated to on the luxurious grounds of Marble Hill Farms. Laundry was strung along makeshift lines and barbed wire fences. A young girl peered at us with large black eyes, through the rusty metal fence, her hands wrapped innocently around its jagged edges.

The side of the road was lined with an assortment of tent-like structures made from pieces of tarpaulins, rusted sheet metal, and pieces of plywood. We learned that the rough structures were housing squatters, recently removed from someone's land. Beds and mattresses were visible on the front porches of most of the houses along the road - people in homes that are barely shacks, offering the homeless somewhere to sleep.

October 28, 2009

Senor Grumpy wore a grin, from ear to ear, as he pulled up to our dock at The Point, a couple of days ago. We knew that his daughter, Angie, who lived in British Columbia, was coming to stay on the island for a while. At once, I knew that the cheerful-looking, blonde woman perched in the front seat of his skiff, was her.

I called John to let him know that we had company, as I took the lines and helped Angie climb out of the boat. The first thing I noticed was her bright, blue eyes. A huge smile lit up her face. She was tall with long legs and wore her wavy, blonde hair cut just above the shoulder. She carried a traveler in her hand, a drink to go, that is, as is common on the island.

"A few of us are heading up to Paya Bay, tomorrow," Mr. Larry told us, after brief introductions. "It's Taco Sunday at the restaurant there. We thought that you and John might like to join us."

We jumped at the chance to explore a little more of the island by land and accepted his invitation. He and Angie Wood returned the next day and met us in Hessie's parking lot, across the canal, in Oak Ridge. Once again, we bounced along the dusty roads of the sparsely populated east end, this time towards Paya Bay Resort.

At the restaurant, we met up with our new-found friends, Mark and Lori. They introduced us to Alex and Kelly, who were their neighbors, they told us, in an island sort of way. That is, their house is in the same Bight, or Bay, as Mark and Lori – Calabash Bight.

Mark and Lori also have family members visiting the island. Lori's daughter, Savannah, and granddaughter, Amyrah, are visiting from Tampa, and are along on this outing to Paya Bay.

Our group was seated on the broad patio, overlooking the sea below on the north side of the island. As we enjoyed delicious chicken, pork, and beef tacos, cold drinks, and fun times with these new friends, I mentioned to John that after two years of never following the road further east than Oak Ridge, we had traveled east twice in less than a week.

Few tourists venture this far east, although there are several resorts and dive centers in the area. There were no tourists at the resort - our group of local gringos were the only customers.

After lunch, we strolled down to the beach. Some of us enjoyed a swim and others stretched out on lounge chairs on the beach and watched.

On the way back, we stopped to pay our respects at a local woman's 83rd birthday party, then once again stopped for a cold *cervesa* at the funny little bar in Spanish Hill. If it has a name, I don't know it. We were entertained by listening to an old anchorage neighbor from West End try to hook up on the phone with his blind date, Isabel. It was a shame we had to leave before she got there, I thought to myself.

Saturday, it was Alex on his guitar and Joe on the spoons across the harbor at BJ's. We joined the usual crowd of gringos that shows up each week. By about 4:00 pm, the musicians had packed up, and we hopped in our dinghy and zipped down to Puky's for a bite to eat.

We inadvertently stumbled into a political party gathering. The captain was edgy and irritated to discover speeches instead of chicken fingers, but I found it interesting and worked hard to keep him in his chair. With speeches finally over, we ordered our dinner to go and enjoyed it on the boat, while watching the sunset.

Strange things happen in the days leading up to an election, here in Roatan. A large powerboat pulled up to a dock across the harbor from us one morning this week, loaded with cheering party supporters. Another huge crowd of party supporters, all dressed in their blue party shirts, climbed on board. The boat raced past us and out they flew, through the cut, going somewhere fast. Where they went I do not know, but they stayed out all night and returned the townsfolk to the dock the next day. Buying votes seems to be an overnight affair here!

Nov 8, 2009

One of my favorite sayings is "Life happens when you had other plans." I announced to the world, or at least to our friends, that I'd be busy day-in and day-out writing my book, with no time for socializing. However, with Lori's daughter, Savannah, and grand-daughter, Amyrah and Larry Wood's daughter, Angie, visiting, it was socializing and not writing, that filled my days.

The outings were numerous. and we were thankful to be included in the group. The final outing, last Thursday, was a visit to Parrot Tree Resort, a large and prestigious gated community on the south coast of the island. It's a gorgeous resort, but oddly, we found there were very few guests there. It felt like our own private resort, as we enjoyed lunch on the beach, and then a swim in the giant pool.

The captain and I ducked out on a party just in time one night at Hayo's Place, in Blue Rock, near Hole in the Wall. Angie was working there and invited us to a birthday party. "It will be great," she told us. "They have a band, free fry pork, and rum."

"You mean fried pork?" I asked her.

"Not here, she told me. Fry pork is what they call it. Island speak."

Having not yet developed the taste for fry pork, we passed on the free hog meat. The free rum, we did not pass on. Later, when Angie said to John and me, "UH OH! The free booze is almost gone," we decided to exit stage left.

The next morning, I emailed Angie and half-joking

asked, "Were there any shots fired or other drama after we left?"

"OH YEAH," she wrote back, "A huge fight broke out, and there were several shots fired. All the women and one gay guy were hiding in the kitchen. A few boats were sunk, and one man was cut with a propeller. You guys left just in time to miss it."

The moral of the story is when you get that feeling here, that it's time to go, IT IS!

The captain is installing a new round of parts that just arrived from Florida, on our 15-hp. dinghy motor. This is an endless task, it seems.

Hurricane Ida left us in peace, and we did not receive any wind or rain. We stocked up on American goodies such as butter and cheese at Eldon's, in French Harbour, and were all set to ride out the storm. Fortunately, instead of a hurricane, we have sunny skies and a calm sea.

Nov 20, 2009

Every Saturday afternoon, Alex and the Lost Boys play music at BJ's Backyard, which is across the water from us, close enough to see from the boat. Last week, Alex, who is a buyer's agent here in Roatan, invited his clients, a couple from Costa Rica, to BJs for the Saturday afternoon fun. We sat with Joe and Joanna, and enjoyed hearing about life in Costa Rica and sharing our feelings about this island.

As we sat down next to the new couple, it was all I could do not to stare at Joanna's tattoo-covered body. Only her face was ink-free. Every other inch of flesh that wasn't covered, and I'm sure a few inches that were, were heavily tattooed. She was a beautiful woman, with long, thick dark hair and bright brown eyes.

Joe was equally unforgettable in appearance. He had a stocky build and a biker-type look. His long, white-blonde hair fell to his shoulders. He sported an equally long, white beard with a matching mustache. His few tattoos seemed mild next to his wife's body art.

"I have a strange request," said Kelly, when she called the following day.

"Joanna, who is a chef and owns a restaurant in Costa Rica, would like to throw a small dinner party in a house they are considering buying. She needs to see if it feels right. She is hoping I can come up with about six people for an impromptu dinner party, and since they met you yesterday, you were the first ones to come to mind. All you have to do is bring the wine."

We jumped at the chance and were picked up at our boat by Alex, Kelly, and Lori.

We were to try to help "sell" the place, which took no effort whatsoever. The house is built in a modular style, divided into different buildings, all situated around a pool and lush tropical gardens. The enormous kitchen with every modern convenience imaginable had room for us to all sit while Joanna whipped up a feast.

Our appetizer was fresh conch salad served in watermelon with delicious homemade tortilla chips. The next course was Cornish hens with fresh pineapple and rosemary. Then we were served fall-off-the-bone ribs baked with rice in coconut milk with savory herbs and fruits.

Retiring to the cozy sun deck, situated off the guest suite, we watched the sun dip below the jungle-covered mountain, taking turns snapping pictures with Alex's new camera.

The asking price for this amazing property is only $450,000 US. It could be had for much less in this struggling market, Alex told us. Tourism is down 70% over last year, and the real estate prices reflect that decline.

Nov 26, 2009

I first met Alana Cooper, who is our neighbor, Jessie Cooper's daughter, when we first arrived in Oak Ridge seven months ago. I met her for the second time at the July 4th party at Miss Sandy's house. However, we didn't really get to know each other until recently. Ironically, it was Alana who introduced me to Lori, whom I now consider a close friend. Lori then brought Alana and me together, and we finally set a date to go horseback riding together.

Alana owns a large piece of property just outside of Oak Ridge. The Cooper family has lived in Roatan for generations. She was born here but educated in the U.S. Like many islanders, she has a husband working and living in the U.S. and two grown daughters there. She has many cousins on the island, I have discovered. I can be telling her a story about an islander I have met, and quite often she says, "Oh he/she is my cousin." Surprise!

I was up at the crack of dawn on Sunday, and John dropped me off at Alana's wharf at 8:00 a.m. It is located across the narrow channel from the Point, on a small piece of waterfront property the family owns. She lives here in the town of Oak Ridge, high up on the hill looking down over the town and the sea, not on her farm, which is a few miles out of town. She longs to live there but prefers to be close to her mother, Aunt Jessie, who is in her 80's. From town, we drove up through the roadside community of Spanish Hill, to the farm.

"Stand back," she said, as I snapped shots of the Brahma Bulls being herded out to pasture for the day. "These are NOT nice bulls." Another field held nicer cows and a few nicer bulls and a couple of horses. More horses were down in the barn, a covered but open-sided structure, for the night. The cattle need to be guarded at night from people who would sneak on to the property to butcher them and make off with the meat.

Jason, his wife, and young baby live and work at the farm, and his young friend James stays as well. Jason bathed and saddled our horses while I had a tour of the farm and snapped photos. About 30 hens and roosters of various colors hung out, in and around the barn, and a large assortment of dogs and cats roamed the grounds.

The farm was not far from the charming little Garifuna

town of Punta Gorda, which lies on the north coast of the island. We have seen it from the bus and the taxi, but a much better view is had from a horse. We stopped partway through town for a cold Salva Vida. The horses, who have no grass at home to speak of, were thrilled to graze nearby, and did not need to be tied up.

James rode with us, acting as our bodyguard. My mount was lively, and I learned that Paso Finos have five gaits. The trademark gait, the Corto (or Paso Corto) is considered the preferred Paso Fino gait. It is what a trot is to other horses and about the same speed. This is the most commonly used gait of the Paso Fino horse, but I was told that my mare had been spoiled and lost this gait.

We continued west after our break, through town, and on to an inviting country road along the beach, surrounded by tropical jungle. After another grazing break, part of the routine, we headed back. I didn't want to stop but knowing how tender my unused thighs would be the next day, I relented, and agreed to return to the farm.

My out of practice legs were sore indeed and bruised on the inside of my knees, but it was a good pain, reminding me of the riding years of my youth. We arrived home with bags of manure and a few plants for my ever-growing collection.

Nov 28, 2009

We celebrated American Thanksgiving on Thursday at Calabash Bight Yacht Club, Kelly and Alex's place. Six Canadians, six Americans, one Dutchman, one turkey, one ham, all the fixings, several pies, and lots of laughs. I came away with a couple of nice plants and some cuttings.

I was even offered a plate of leftovers, or a take-away plate, which is a custom here on the island. Our friends were loading up plates for their watchies (house-sitters) and offered us a plate, which was much appreciated. Nothing tastes better than leftover turkey.

"Look, honey. I found the bullet that killed the pig," I said, as I enjoyed my takeaway plate the next day for lunch.

The captain laughed when I showed him the silver bullet.

"That's the missing end to Lori's meat thermometer," he said. Lori had asked Kelly to watch for it in the soup she was planning to make from the ham bone, having no idea it had traveled all the way to Oak Ridge in my leftovers. Mark picked it up the next day.

Our pot-luck donation was two home-made pies - one pumpkin and one cherry. "We need to buy Cool Whip to go with the pies," I told John, a few days ago. Our search began in Coxen Hole, where there was no Cool Whip to be found. Our favorite little lunch place in Coxen Hole was closed, but we found an even better spot, right beside the cruise ships. Local prices, one of my favorite local musicians, and lots of happy tourists made for a fun time.

I was encouraged to see two ships in port that day. John saw three yesterday, two at the downtown Coxen Hole terminal, and one at the new Mahogany Bay terminal, which just opened this week.

Nov 29, 2009

Today began like no other Sunday since we have been in Oak Ridge. I heard horns tooting before dawn as workers arrived at the voting polls, which open at 6:00 a.m. Normally on Sunday morning, there is no boat traffic passing by, making it remarkably quiet and peaceful. However, on Election Day, water taxis flying the red and white Liberal and blue and white National party flags filed past constantly.

It is more like a sporting event than an election, with voters dressed in red or blue, according to their party affiliations. The taxi fares are pre-paid by the two political parties to make sure everyone gets out to vote.

In town, the road traffic was much the same. Families turned out in their Sunday finest, poured out of taxis. Red or blue - shame on you if you take the wrong one, which would be difficult to do since they are decorated with party posters. All over town, barbeques were set up. Giant speakers were unloaded from pick-up trucks. Let the party begin!

Nobody scurried into the polling station and back out to their car to resume their busy life like we do back at home. This was an all-day affair.

Dec 4, 2009

It has been almost a week since the election, and the parties continue. The winning party hosts a huge pig or beef roast in a different community each night, as a thank you to the voters. Meals and drinks are *gratis*. Enormous speakers pump out music so loud, you feel it as well as hear it.

When the results started pouring in on Monday night, we could hear the cheering of hundreds of people, still in town a day after the election, to await results and for the winning party to celebrate their win. Just as the captain and I crawled into bed, the loud music began. We have been warned that election time is not the best time for gringos to go out at night, so we have laid low this past week.

The days and weeks fly by here in Roatan and Old Man Winter has found us. There is no hiding from him. There are no snow drifts like we see at home, but we do have cold fronts tear through, making even me feel glad for short periods of time that I am docked and not tearing my hair out at anchor.

Ironically, my friend Jeannie, who loves shore and all that comes with it, is braving the windy anchorage at French Harbour, testing their brand new 66 lb Bruce anchor, which so far has passed with flying colors. No more drag races in the middle of the night for the folks on Oasis (knock on wood). No more pointing the flashlight to attempt to help them, only to see the full moon (oh no that's Jim's bare ass) and hear John say,

149

"Honey, I don't think that is helping."

Tucked away safe and sound here in Oak Ridge, we hear the wind screaming through at night, flinging sideways rain at us so that I have to get up, navigate around the big fan that stands at the end of our bed, trying not to wake the captain, to close and lock our side port-hole windows to keep the rain out.

Then around 5:00 am, the luz (or power) goes out. The wave of heat when the fan stops wakes me. Once again, I get up, unplug the fan from the electrical outlet, plug it into the extension cord that runs through the galley, up the steps, and into the inverter up in the main cabin. I flip on the inverter, working quickly, before the captain, also, has a rude awakening.

About a month ago, my trusty old video camera was stolen from my office up in the house, here on Oak Ridge Point. The book project screeched to a halt. I have my logs to work from. However, my videotapes of our travels, which I watch each day, as I write, cannot be played. The millions of priceless details that I was able to recall by watching the movies of our cruises, were lost.

It was an old, second-hand camera I have been using. It replaced one that I had used earlier in our travels, which was compatible. There was no such camera for sale on this island. There was not even the same camera on sale online, anywhere. That is how old it was.

Feeling discouraged, I told my sad tale to the gang down at Hole in the Wall, one afternoon.

"I think I have the same camera," said our friend Bob, from *s/v Bettie*, as we nursed our cold beers on the deck of the local happy hour hangout.

"I just got a new camera," Bob told me. "The one I've been using is a spare now. The spare I had previously would be an extra spare. You are welcome to it."

I am thrilled to be the new owner of the extra spare camera, with a bag full of accessories. It is much better than my old one, yet totally compatible, and I am back at the book with a vengeance.

The camera came with an underwater housing, a dream come true for me. I have longed to film underwater for years and now, once this wind settles a little, I can do it!

It also came with an extra wide-angle lens and 2x converter lens, cables, chargers, and batteries It feels like Santa Claus has come early to Oak Ridge Point!

The odd little roadside bar in Spanish Hill

Watching from the sidelines

Nothing but the finest stemware for Miss Angie Wood

Captain John, driving the dinghy

Sunday "Taco Day" at Paya Bay Resort

Kelly, demonstrating the upside-down labels on the cranberry tins

Lori, stirring the gravy

The beautiful pool at Parrot Tree Resort

Election day – Red party supporters heading to the polls.

A dory taking a blue party supporter to vote.

Sunset in Oak Ridge, seen from the back deck of *Diamond Lil*

Horseback riding on the beach in Punta Gorda

Chapter 9

Nov 11, 2010

Captain John and I are alive and well. *Diamond Lil* is still tied to the dock at Oak Ridge Point. Our three-month stay has morphed into a year and seven months.

I spent the last year working on my first book, The Captain's Log - Diamond Lil does the Loop. I have had the use of the house here at the Point as my office, and I would challenge anyone to find a more inspirational setting to write. Papa John passed away last winter. We miss the smile on his face as he stops outside *Diamond Lil* to smell the flowers we have growing. The planters John built are a burst of color, as we continue to put down roots here.

We are still afloat, stuck in what a friend of ours refers to as a 'sticky harbor'. I am not referring to any physical substance in the water, although we do have plenty of that floating by, but to a certain type of place to which many people come and fewer people leave. We are part of a large and constantly growing group of ex-pats, who came here once upon a time, by boat or by plane, fell in love with the place, and stayed.

Nov 18, 2010

Hurricane season officially begins June 1st and lasts until November 30th. We cruised all the way back to the safety of Canada for our first hurricane season. We spent the next two hurricane seasons tucked safely up the Rio Dulce in Guatemala, Central America's favorite hurricane hole. After that, we elected to stay put in Roatan. Many of our fellow cruisers opt to leave the Bay

Islands and find refuge in the Rio, and now, as hurricane season ends, we welcome them back for the winter.

Some are here for six months. Others are passing through on their way to exotic locations such as the San Andres Islands, off Columbia. Some are heading through the Panama Canal, like Jim and Jeanie, on their way to the Sea of Cortez on Mexico's North West coast. We will catch up on the news as they pass by. We'll ask about our old friends in the Rio, and they'll ask about the tropical storms we experienced here.

Most tropical storms pass to the northeast of the Bay Islands. Historically, it's a much safer bet than most Caribbean islands. There are exceptions and hurricanes do occasionally strike here. Mitch (1993) is the most well-known of the Bay Islands hurricanes, hovering over the sister island of Guanaja for days, causing extensive damage.

Captain John and I have had three brushes with tropical storms this season. Typically, the talk starts five or six days before the storm hits, as we all watch it form and cross the Atlantic. The first order of business each day, well the second, after the kettle goes on for coffee, is opening our laptops. NOAA is just one of the weather nets we check. Facebook is quicker because all our friends are watching also, and an approaching tropical storm becomes the topic of the day.

If the mainland of Honduras is hit and the roads and ports on the north coast are damaged, the ships that bring everything over to the island won't run. We drove down to French Harbour, where all the large, modern grocery stores are located and stocked up on basics - coffee, milk, sugar, etc. Power can be out for days or weeks, resulting in banks being closed, so we stocked up on cash as well.

We filled two five-gallon jugs with diesel fuel for the generator on the property because power outages are a given. We loaded everything from the car into *El Tanko,* the boat we use to get back and forth from the Point to town, and then unloaded it all onto the narrow dock in the boathouse and hauled it over to *Diamond Lil.*

In our own town of Oak Ridge, we loaded up on 5-gallon jugs of drinking water and any of the supplies that we can get here. The shelves empty quickly as everyone does the same thing. John makes sure the generator will start. As the storm draws nearer, the boaters ask each other, "Are you staying or moving?"

The large shrimp and lobster boats begin to trickle in, docking across the waterway from us at the shrimp factory where they unload their cargo. Then they leave the dock to seek refuge. Many of them head to Calabash Bight. We see the pictures on Facebook. We watch closely. They are our first clue as to what the locals expect. When they start tucking these giant vessels into the mangroves, we pay attention.

Decision day. The storm is about a day away. If we move the boat, we want to do it by daylight. We prefer not to move it unless it is necessary. Which way will the wind come from, we wonder? If it comes from the southwest, we will be pushed away from the dock, which is not a bad thing.

If the wind comes from the northeast or north, we will be pushed onto the dock, which isn't appealing. In the case of this eventuality, we dropped two anchors out in the channel, with lines left loose until the storm arrives. Then, we will loosen the lines tying us to shore, pull away from the dock, and count on these anchors to hold us. We added extra lines from the boat to the shore as well.

We anchored Roatan Joe's catamaran, *Lana Kai*, in much the same way, so she wouldn't be tossed forward into *La Feets*, the little shed that serves as a laundry/workroom. We also tied her to a tree onshore.

The captain cooked a large pot of chili, so we will have plenty of food. All our friends are doing the same thing, cooking hurricane food before the storm arrives. We are ready - the storm will hit during the night, so I try to prepare with an afternoon nap. Facebook is a flurry of activity. Our friends are as nervous as we are.

Our elderly neighbor, Miss Jessie, packs up and heads high up the hill to her daughter Alana's house. "We will keep an eye on your place," we tell her.

Our other neighbor, Lourdes, who speaks no English, comes by in her boat, and we exchange phone numbers. I tell her to put her boat in our boathouse for the night, so it won't fill with rainwater.

The winds are building as we crawl into bed, but we try to get a little sleep. The forecast calls for the storm to veer north, but we will still expect a lot of wind and rain. The boat tosses back and forth in the wind. There is no sleeping on your side - you must lie on your back or be rolled around. We're used to it though, and we fall asleep.

It is not the storm, but the sound of about eight screaming diesel engines fighting 60-mile an hour winds that wake us up at about 4:00 a.m.

"Oh no," I moan. This must mean that the storm is going to hit us after all. Where are they going in the middle of the night? My worst fear is moving the boat in dangerous weather in the dark of night.

We shine our flashlight on the mayhem in the water beside us. *Proton*, a large government boat, has been at the dock for a year and a half - she never moves, but I hear her engine cough and come to life. Boats, still rafted together, three-wide, are floating not far from us. Men scramble about their decks, yelling and screaming.

"Look, they have pulled the dock away," says John. Sure enough, the dock that about eight large boats were tied to has been ripped away, and large chunks of it are still tied to some of them. With flashlights in hand, we watched the fiasco long enough to make sure we were not caught up in the tangle of boats. Before long, they all disappeared to find refuge somewhere else, and we returned to bed.

We woke to a property flooded by rain and strewn with

debris from the storm surge, but Matthew has passed as a only a tropical storm. I took some pictures to send to Roatan Joe. We walked over to check on Miss Jessie's house. It is fine. There is no damage, but her property is a mess, so I took some pictures there too.

Three weeks later, we are glad we left the storm anchors out and just loosened off the lines. Paula is headed our way. We go through the same routine. Once again, we wake to find we have been spared. She has veered off to the north to ruin someone else's day.

Just over another week passes. Things come in threes, I tell the captain. Let's leave the storm anchors out. Richard looms, and this one really has everyone talking. John goes over to Hessie's, the little store directly across from us, and the owner, Darcy, tells him that this one is coming! The fishing fleet is on its way in!

The good news is that the docks across from us are not repaired, so we have no more fishing fleet to worry about slamming into us. Once again, we haul all the plants that are in pots to safety in *La Feets* and the cistern room in the house. We ferry Miss Jessie and her two little dogs across to Alana's dock so that once again she can spend the night safely up the hill.

The storm is predicted to hit in the early hours of the morning. Before turning in for the night, we once again tighten the storm anchor lines and loosen the lines to shore. Once we do this, there is no getting off the boat. We wait. Richard is only a category 1, but more than enough excitement for me. Our anchors hold, and we suffer no damage. Once the morning comes and John can see, he checks on Miss Jessie's house and returns to the boat looking for a long line to tie down a large corner of her roof which is flapping in the wind.

I follow him over, both of us in our heavy yellow raincoats, and watch as he lassoes the corner of her roof and ties it down. The worst is over. The storm is diminishing. John stands inside the open window of the big house to shoot photographs of waves higher than buildings.

The tree that *Lana Kai* was tied to has been ripped from the ground and has pulled the port side bow of *Lana Kai* into *La Feets,* the building in front of us. John cuts the line with a knife, and the boat snaps back into place. We survey the damage, and consider ourselves lucky once again.

Dec 7, 2010

The signs that Christmas is growing near are subtle in Roatan. After five years of futile efforts, I have finally convinced the captain to allow me to decorate *Diamond Lil* with Christmas lights. I also wound a string of lights around the trunk of a large palm tree on our lawn.

The first night we plugged the lights in, we could hear the children from Pandy Town across the Bight gather on the shore to ooh and aah. Life is very simple here, and they were content to stay there for hours, until we turned the lights off, which I did early, feeling guilty for sending these poor little children home to ask their struggling families when Santa is coming.

While the lights were on, several boats stopped outside *Diamond Lil.* We heard Spanish words. We know several of them, but had we not, it would not matter. Some things transcend language. Life is simple here.

Both fireworks - not pretty, sparkly ones like in Canada, but loud, bomb-like ones, and gunfire are not uncommon sounds at night. I had to laugh after our colorful lights went on for the first time. We heard a couple of shots, and John said, "Oh great, a new target." We are lit up like the old Eaton's store in downtown Toronto.

The next day, my friend, Eulina, told me that she took her mother to church, and that in his sermon the pastor denounced the use of Christmas lights as a waste of money, contributing to the coffers of RECO. The despised electric company charges rates higher than what we pay in Canada, to people who earn a fraction of what we do back home.

I asked my friend, "Do you like the lights?" and she said, "Oh yes girl. I love them. You leave them up. They are beautiful."

We sat out on our back deck and watched the pretty lights reflecting, not in snow, like I grew up with, but in the water. Sorry, Pastor.

Many of the ex-pats and cruisers who come to Roatan like to give back to the community in various ways. There are a group of American doctors called The

Floating Doctors, who arrived recently after a stint in Haiti. They are dispensing free health care and thousands of dollars of supplies to needy islanders.

My friend Pat, here on her sailboat from Pennsylvania with her husband Randy, is an RN and she has been volunteering at the medical clinic that The Floating Doctors are conducting in our town of Oak Ridge. She loves the work, and the stories she tells me are unbelievable. Ignorance runs rampant. Babies receive coca-cola in their bottles, and diabetes is prevalent. Many women believe that they need an antibiotic shot after each period. These are just a few examples of the medical challenges the islanders face.

Pat enjoys her work and got us involved with another project, cleaning and repainting the school that our friend, Norma Morales, teaches at. Norma is a wonderful, warm Honduran woman who married our Canadian friend, Mr. Larry, from BC, a few months ago.

We arrive to find a tiny, two-room schoolhouse that serves children from grades 1-6, and a separate, even smaller, kindergarten room. A huge pile of garbage that the tide continually washes in is piled behind the buildings, in what serves as a school ground.

We spent the entire first day clearing, scraping, and sanding the walls, and cleaning the yard. A huge pile of garbage was taken away when we were done.

The walls inside one of the two rooms had been painted in dismal shades of dark red and yellow. On the second workday, the dark walls were repainted with a lighter color, which helped to brighten the tiny rooms and make them seem a little larger.

Dec 21, 2010

Last Friday, the gift-wrapping party was held at BJ's Backyard, in conjunction with the Banditos' weekly live performance. The band, originally named Alex and the Lost Boys, played each Saturday afternoon. We have Alex, Mike, Joe, and Keith. Alex and Mike play the guitar, and Keith and Joe join in on percussion. Joe has a special way with his spoons. Alex, Mike, and Joe all sing.

Guest performers are always welcome to join the band. This makes for even more fun as regulars and tourists alike get up to entertain the crowd.

Because Alex also has a busy real estate business, with Saturday being his busiest day, the weekly musical event has been changed from Saturday to Friday.

A record crowd showed up for the wrapping party, groups of gringos arriving with bags of gifts, mostly purchased back in the US and Canada. We are all asked to donate as many small, dollar-store type gifts as we can physically carry back to the island.

The challenge is finding room in our bags when we fly back to the island since we all try to shop for things we cannot find here. Everyone found room for some gifts for the needy children, many of whom would otherwise not wake up to find anything from Santa on Christmas morning.

We take for granted back in our land of plenty that
Santa will come. Here there is no such certainty for the
children. Kelly told me about a local woman with six
children. All she could manage to buy were three shiny,
red apples on Christmas Eve - half an apple for each
child. The story got Kelly thinking about how we could
help brighten up Christmas Day for some of these
people in our community.

This is just one way to make a difference. We can't help
each child on the island, but we try to bring a little
pleasure to a few. Expats do this all over the island, in
different communities. We are happy to give back a
little to these people who graciously welcome us into
their homeland.

Dec 23, 2010

Despite the rainy day, the annual children's party in
Fiddler's Bight was a tremendous success. Sixty or more
children showed up, as well as parents of younger
children. Imagine the delight when each child was
greeted with a noisy horn, a bottle of bubbles to blow,
and a colorful mask to wear.

Early in the festivities, a Santa piñata was raised into a
tree, and the game began. I expected chaos, but I was
amazed by how organized the game was. A group of
teenage boys worked the piñata, pulling it up off the
ground and lowering it as the need arose, making sure it

didn't come open before each child had a turn bashing poor Santa.

The smallest children went first, some so young that they needed help holding the stick. By the time the older children got their hands on the stick, poor Saint Nick was falling apart. Each time a few candies fell from the piñata, the crowd of children scrambled to get them. When this happened, an adult quickly clutched the child with the stick in hand, who was intent on whacking Santa and not noticing the pile of kids on the ground below.

Finally, when the candies poured out of the piñata, the kids went wild. Mothers rushed forward into the melee to rescue their charges from the pile of bodies. I truly feared for the ones on the bottom. This is a very rough game, but part of the culture here.

Next, a meager lunch of rice, cake, and fruit juice was served. Once two orderly lines were formed, one of the girls, and one of the boys, ranging from youngest to oldest, the serving began. A hush fell over the crowd as the children ate. No child here needs to be told to clean their plate.

After lunch, the Church Lady read the kids a bible story. The story was followed by the hula-hoop contest. The kids grew more and more excited as the climax of the party, gift time, arrived. Each child received several gifts. Few children opened them. Mothers bagged them and took them home. The kids were thrilled with all their gifts, opened and unopened alike.

As I handed a second gift to one young boy, he smiled up at me and said, "That's ok Ma'am. I already have one!"

Dec 30, 2010

Cultural differences that we live with day to day here in Roatan are especially evident on holidays. Christmas is no exception, and as John and I drove down island to do our weekly shopping and pick up a few last-minute items on the morning of the 24th, we were once again struck by some of the differences.

The lack of commercialism is the biggest difference, but even this is changing over the years. The new Mega Mall and the new Eldon's store in French Harbour carry more Christmas decorations, food, and gifts each year. However, it is still a fraction of what is available in Canada or the U.S.

Fishing fleets return for the holidays. Fishermen are thick in the pocketbook with their pay, and parties are in full swing. Employees receive, or are supposed to receive, what is referred to as the 13th pay, a month's salary, is to be paid in December. It is meant as a form of holiday pay for employees.

Less emphasis is placed on the actual 25th. Children don't necessarily receive their gifts on that day, but over the course of the week. Out of our boat windows, we witnessed a parade of dories passing by with electric cars and other shiny new gifts. We ran into friends of ours whose son was choosing his gift from the displays in the stores rather than receiving it as a surprise from

Santa.

The different groups on the island also celebrate in different ways. Most of the celebration seems to take place during the evening and night of December 24th. Stores close early, around 1:00 pm, and the party begins and carries on until dawn. Fireworks are huge, and when they run out the odd pistol shot can be heard. These are in stark contrast to the sounds we hear on Christmas Eve, in Canada.

We joined friends down at Hole in the Wall at 3:00 in the afternoon. After weeks of looking for eggnog, Pat decided to make her own, and she brought it to share with the gang. Bob served appetizers for the local gringo crowd that stops by after the tourists leave. We don't often eat the $25.00, all-you-can-eat buffet like the tourists do, so it was a treat to nibble on succulent pieces of melt-in-your-mouth beef and lobster.

At home in the boat, we tuned in to our local radio station, the one and only station, but there were no Christmas carols to be heard. I complained about how I had always listened to Christmas carols on Christmas Eve growing up, as we turned in for the night.

Be careful what you wish for, my mother used to always warn me, and she was right because at 3:30 in the morning I got my Christmas carols. Right outside our boat, making their rounds, the carolers banged drums and hooted on horns and sang O Little Town of Bethlehem to a reggae beat. Every half hour, we were woken by fireworks and partiers. When I crawled out of bed behind the captain at 6:00 a.m., my eyes had that scratchy feeling that I remembered from the years of small children waking up, just hours after Santa had crawled to bed.

I baked two pumpkin pies. John stuffed the turkey, and got it in the oven. We were invited to Miss Jessie's for an early dinner, around 1:00 pm, so we needed an early start.

We enjoyed coffee and exchanged a few simple gifts we had bought each other. There isn't much shopping here on the island unless you want t-shirts or souvenirs. John cooked a Christmas breakfast of bacon, eggs, toast, and pancakes.

I am enjoying my gardening tools, pruning shears, and seeds from the new Ace Hardware store. These are just a few of the things that were previously difficult to find if not unavailable on the island. I also got a wood-burning kit, to use on the driftwood paintings I have been making.

Regardless of the agreed-upon 1:00 pm start time, if there is anything you can count on here, it's that everything will be late. We were therefore not surprised when Alana called just after 12:00 pm, to say they were running behind schedule. It was a relief to us, for much like the islanders, we hate to rush.

We carried our turkey next door around 2: 00 pm. Mark and Douglas helped us cart over chairs, gravy, a sharp knife, some ice, and eggnog. I found the eggnog at

Eldon's on Christmas Eve Day. I had been asking for eggnog. Silly me! Here, they call it *ron popo*. Once I remembered that I spied it in the dairy section and snatched up several small boxes.

John carved the turkeys and we helped ourselves to a holiday buffet and spread out around Miss Jessie's island home to enjoy our meal. There were 11 of us - Miss Jessie, her daughter Miss Alana, Miss Sandy, from part-way down the point, Miss Bev from here in Oak Ridge, Douglas Cooper, Miss Jessie's grandson, also from Oak Ridge, Mark, and Lori, from Calabash Bight and their neighbor Roger, Mark and his son Hunter, also from our Point, and John and me.

When an islander addresses a woman older than himself/herself, she is called Miss. When a member of the younger generation addresses an older man, the title 'Mr.,' as in 'Mr. John' is likewise used. The words "ma'am" and "sir" are also used, as a sign of respect for their elders.

After the main course, we indulged in cherry, peach, and pumpkin pie, topped with Cool Whip. After a little post-meal conversation, we strolled the short distance, across the narrow point, to our boat.

I brought my turkey carcass home with me. There was enough turkey left on it for a few leftovers and some soup broth. John uses it to make his delicious French onion soup.

From left to right – Mike, Alex, and Joe – the Banditos

BJ – owner and manager of BJ's Backyard in Oak Ridge

The Great Room, where I began working on my book

Conch shells weighing down my papers in my office.

The property on Oak Ridge Point, after Hurricane Richard

Miss Jessie's house on The Point, with a corner of the roof tied down

Raising the Santa pinata at the Children's Christmas party

A happy boy, posing for me at the Children's Christmas party

Our dockside garden, thriving in the planters that John made.

Enjoying our Christmas dinner at Miss Jessie's house on the Point

Chapter 10

January 1, 2011

For the second year in a row, we rang in the New Year in Roatan. Last year, we spent New Year's Eve at Hole in the Wall, in Blue Rock, celebrating at 6:00 pm, since none of our friends expected to stay up until midnight.

This New Year's Eve was equally tame. We crossed the soft grass on Joe's property and let ourselves out of the yard through the back gate, juggling bags and dishes with our pot-luck offerings. From there, we strolled along the white sand walkway behind Miss Jessie's house. Passing her place, we followed the heaved and cracked strip of pavement that serves as a sidewalk along the south shore of this narrow spit of land.

At times, the raised walkway, only a couple of feet wide, has no land on either side, but only water. At certain times of the year, when the tide is at its highest or a storm is raging, the water rises over the walkway, making it a treacherous walk. Our destination was Miss Sandy's place, where we were invited for New Year's Eve drinks. It was a tame crowd, the usual group of neighbors. We were home by 7:30 pm, and I was in bed, reading, by 9:00 pm.

Although we didn't see midnight, we did hear it, through the open hatch above our cozy bed. As on Christmas Eve, we were kept awake by the sounds of fireworks exploding and revelers carrying on ALL night long. Surely the firework supplies must be dwindling, we tell ourselves. Soon it will be time to wash the salt off our Christmas lights and remove them from *Diamond Lil*.

A New Year's Day lunch at the Crow's Nest Restaurant at Marble Hill Farms, thanks to a suggestion posted on Facebook by one of the gang last week, was a festive beginning to 2011.

"Hey, Mel," shouted Rebecca, from behind the bar, as we entered the open-sided restaurant. Rb, as she likes to be called, was a tall, leggy black girl, a real head-turner. One of our friends once said that every man on the island was secretly in love with Rb, along with a few of the women.

"There's trouble," said John, as she looked up from her work, grinning a mischievous grin and looking as cute as ever in her short white shorts and snug blue and white striped tank top.

"JOHN," she said, trying to sound stern, pretending to be annoyed by the verbal abuse he routinely dishes out. The smile that lit up her face told the truth - that she enjoyed the game as much as him.

Her better half, Bryan, stood quietly behind the bar, greeting us with a nod and a quiet hello. At first, they seem like an odd couple, but once you get to know them, that changes. Bryan is older, and he is white. He wears his hair clipped short, perhaps because his hairline is receding a little. He speaks quietly and slowly and when he smiles, dimples light up his face. He seems content and amused by life, for he is always smiling.

January 3, 2011

At 8:10 am, the sky is clear, and the sun is shining. The air is cool and fresh, with the temperature expected to only reach 82 degrees F, today.

Directly across from me, out my starboard-side windows, I have a view of Roatan Joe's house, with the sun streaming across the palm trees on the lawn. There is almost no breeze and a light coating of dew sparkles in the sun on our plants and flowers.

Reflections from the sun on the wavelets ripple across the boathouse, to my right. Behind me, out my port-side window, I hear the racket of dories coming and going in the morning rush hour. From our back window, behind where John sits, I see the woman who works at the tiny *gasolinera* on our neighbor's dock being dropped off to open her tiny gas station for the day. She is an attractive Spanish woman who sits perched in her small building all day long with her laptop on her lap, listening to music and doing the things that we all do every day on our computers. When Roatan Joe arrives and password protects our modem, she'll be bored to death, I suspect.

My first order of business today is to drive from Oak Ridge, up through Spanish Hill, to a new grocery store called Roymart. I need to buy a graham cracker pie-shell to make a key lime pie for the dinner party we are invited to tonight. I have already searched through the *tiendas* in Oak Ridge, and there is not a pie shell to be had.

Before Roymart opened, we would have an hour-long drive down-island to buy such a thing. After dinner, a group of our friends plan to go dancing at Hayo's Place, a little bar down in Blue Rock. It will be a late-night for us, compared to our usual bedtime of 8:00 or 9:00 pm.

Feb 7, 2011

The port-side transmission has been repaired. Our hydraulic steering seal has been replaced. The oil has been changed, the batteries checked, and a faulty cable replaced. The boat bottom was cleaned, and the fridge defrosted. A switch for our windlass, which could not be repaired, has been ordered and shipped to Lisa's house. She arrives a week from today, and that is warp-speed compared to trying to have something shipped to Roatan.

The anchors that went down in hurricane season have come up - not a pretty sight. We bought a new three-burner, table-top propane stove and the hose to hook it to the propane tank.

Our propane tank, barbeque, deckchairs, and John's tools have been hauled from *La Feets*, the little shed here at the Point.

I watered my flowers one last time. We zipped across to Hessie's for a few last-minute groceries. Ice, beer, and soft drinks have been stowed. Our power line has been disconnected, the lines from shore untied, and we are off.

It's been a while, and the waiting has made our trip

even sweeter. Nothing beats the open sea, even if it's only a five or six-mile trip and before we knew it, we were there. Our destination - Port Royal – at the quiet, unspoiled east end of the island, most of which is accessible only by water.

I think back to the first time we dropped our hook in Port Royal when we didn't know a soul on this island. This time, we were barely settled before friends Kim and Joe Wonder hailed us on the VHF radio to invite us up to their home, near where we were anchored, for a beer.

Because our windlass is not functioning, we asked friends Ed and Julie if we could tie to the mooring ball that they installed by the landmark 'cow and calf' rocks in Port Royal to use for their charter catamaran business.

Ed and Julie, originally from Canada, can barely keep up with the demand for their unique excursions. They offer a variety of charter options, including half and full-day sails that cater to cruise ship visitors, and longer trips for those lucky enough to spend more time in the Bay Islands. Once in a while, they offer an ex-pat cruise. The ex-pat cruise is one available to friends and guests of friends, for half of the regular price.

Ed and Julie have guests from Canada on board, who donated time to provide health care over in the barrios on the mainland. Their reward, once their work on the mainland was done, is a little vacation time on our island.

Ed called a few friends and neighbors, and before long, we had company. *S/V Free Radical* arrived in Port Royal and put down an anchor since we were on their mooring ball. They had a crowd on board and before long others from the Port Royal area joined the party, tying their *pangas* and skiffs to *S/V Free Radical*.

I swam over from *Diamond Lil*. John loaded my beachwear, my camera, and a few cold beers into the skiff and joined us. Ed and Julie treated us all to lunch aboard and a great afternoon.

Sunday morning, we untied from the mooring ball and retraced our route, stopping at Mark and Lori's place, Turtlegrass Marina. We have been invited to their Super Bowl party. We tied *Diamond Lil* to one of their mooring balls, took the skiff to shore, and climbed the 79 stairs to their home. High above the jungle and the sparkling blue water of Calabash Bight, we had a bird's eye view of *Diamond Lil* below. When guests arrived and asked where we lived, I was proud to point to our vessel. I felt happy to be one of the 'boat people' once again, even if only for the weekend.

Feb 14, 2011

"We're booked!" read the subject line in an email I received a few weeks ago from my long-time friend, Lisa Brewster.

Lisa and I became friends when I was 19 years old, and she was 17. We met at Southam Murray Printing, in Toronto, where we both began our printing careers. I was a payroll clerk, and she was a film filing clerk. We were probably the two lowest-paid employees in the place at that time. We each rented a small apartment in the Bathurst and Wilson area of Toronto. Mine was above a used bookstore, beside a Jewish bakery. Hers was in the basement of a house.

I had a car - a little Toyota Corolla. Lisa didn't. So, each morning, I would pick her up, drive her to work, and then back home again at the end of our day. She attended our 10:00 am coffee break in the payroll office, along with a group of four or five girls. We often ate lunch together. We again enjoyed the 3:00 pm coffee break in the payroll office.

We bowled with a group of coworkers each Wednesday after work. Then we went dancing to Disco music at the Gypsy Gypsy at the Holiday Inn beside the Yorkdale Mall. We nicknamed it the Tipsy Tipsy. We often spent our weekends and holidays together. We played baseball once a week during the summer hours – again with our coworkers. They were good days.

Now, 35 years later, Lisa is coming to visit us in Roatan for the first time. She is bringing Betty - a neighbor from her previous home, with whom she has become friends. They were due to land on Valentine's Day, she told me. I told her to expect the unexpected when you come to the island.

"Oh no," I said to John when I woke this morning to the sound of torrential rain and crawled out of bed to look outside.

"This is not good. What if the plane can't land?" I moaned.

"You worry too much," said hubby. "Come on. Let's get ready. We might need extra time to get there if the roads are this wet."

I cursed the weather as we dug out our foul weather gear and packed some large garbage bags to wrap our guests' luggage in. We had to travel from the airport to the car, the car to our skiff, and across the waterway to the dock, then into the house, with their suitcases.

Sure enough, torrential rainfall closed the Roatan airport, literally, as their plane attempted to land. We heard the roar of jet engines as the landing was attempted. However, we soon learned that the landing had been aborted, due to zero visibility on the short, single runway at our quaint little airport.

We stood, shaking our heads, trying to get information - not an easy feat in Roatan. We finally learned that our guests had flown to Belize, where they landed and sat on the runway for an hour. Upon returning to Roatan, the pilot announced over the radio that they would be making another "attempt" to land, Lisa told me, when she finally arrived.

"When he made that announcement, I wondered how many attempts we would have to make. I'm glad it was only two."

We sat outside, in front of the airport, soaking up the sun while the girls recharged the nicotine levels in their bloodstreams. Their last cigarette outside the airport in the chilly winter air of Toronto at 4 a.m. seemed like a distant memory, Lisa told me. The flight down, the aborted landing, the flight to Belize, the hour on the runway in Belize, the flight back to Roatan, and the wait in the immigration line had made for a very long morning.

"I wondered, as I sat on the runway in Belize," she told me, "how the frozen steaks I had tucked into my luggage at 3:00 am last night, were faring."

We packed into Joe's small burgundy Toyota, and headed for the east end of the island to our little town of Oak Ridge. A stop at BJ's was necessary while John bailed the water from the boat, and we waited for the heavy rain to stop. A second bailing was necessary before we finally made it home and unloaded our guests and their luggage on to a foot-wide dock in the boathouse with two excited dogs running around their feet.

"You mean we have to get in this boat every time we go somewhere?" Betty asked. Lisa had warned me that her friend didn't like boats, which was evident on this first day. By day four, I told someone that Betty didn't like boats, and she piped up, "I DO NOW!"

Living here with us in Water World for a week, we made a boater out of Betty and an islander out of Lisa. The captain taxied and ferried us around all week and waited patiently while we laid on beaches and beside pools and shopped for souvenirs. He spoiled us with his great cooking while we enjoyed a whirlwind week.

I guess we played too hard because we both came down with a head cold and flu bug and spent the next week recuperating. We're finally back to normal, well normal for someone who lives here in Roatan that is. Now that we are back to our regular quiet routine, which is quite different than the busy, social week we enjoyed with Lisa and Betty, the fact that I have not yet found a publisher for my book is beginning to plague me.

What to do? Persist with finding a publisher and/or literary agent, waiting month after month for a stream of rejection letters with the hope that one day I'll find "the one" or to self-publish and market the book myself. I just don't know what to do.

Mar 14, 2011

When the captain asked me what I wanted for my birthday this year, I told him, "Honey, I don't need a thing. This trip to Guanaja that we are planning is the best gift I could think of."

Angie Wood had planned a boat trip to Guanaja, another of the Honduras Bay Islands, about 50 miles east of Roatan. She had such a good response that the boat taking the tour was full, and she wanted to know if we would like to ferry a few left-over travelers in *Diamond Lil*. There were 30 people from the island going, many of whom are our friends. Suffice to say she did not need to twist my arm.

We cast off from the dock at The Point, crossing the short waterway to BJs on the other side. In torrential rain, we picked up our guests. We had three people join us on *Diamond Lil* - John and Linda Butler and their friend, Mark, who is visiting the island. It was our first time meeting them.

John and Linda are ex-pats, originally from Connecticut, whose island home is in Punta Blanca. John co-owns and manages an automobile maintenance, repair service, and used car business. Linda is a nurse. They hope to retire in a few years and spend more time on the island. This winter, John is visiting for six weeks. Linda is only here for two weeks.

John burst on to the deck of *Diamond Lil*, gushing with enthusiasm about the trip, despite the soggy circumstances.

He was of medium height, with medium length sandy brown hair, slightly greying. He wore matching facial hair and an enormous smile. Behind his flashy sunglasses, he had the freshly tanned look of a sun-seeker that had been away too long. His smile was broad and contagious, radiating from his blue eyes as well as his face. His most noticeable feature, however, was his voice. It had a booming, musical quality, as if he had swallowed an amplifier.

Linda struck me at first as an odd match for John. She was petite, with dark reddish-brown, fashionably styled hair and blue eyes. She was pretty in a cute, pixie-like fashion, with a small face and delicate features. She was as soft-spoken and demure as John was outgoing and vivacious.

John and his friend, Mark, perched on the bow of the boat as the skies miraculously cleared for our trip. Linda seated herself on the settee in the main cabin, curled up comfortably inside.

Our arrival in Guanaja, four hours later, was likewise in torrential rain. The visibility was so poor that we had no choice but to idle outside the harbor, waiting for the rain to slow, to see the channel markers.

Once the skies cleared, we enjoyed ferrying a boatload of people from Bonacca – the main community in Guanaja - over to the Manati Restaurant and Bar, in El Bight, where 26 of us were meeting for dinner. There were people upstairs in the flybridge, people downstairs, inside, outside, and on the bow. It was a record number of passengers on *Diamond Lil.*

Apr 15, 2011

The wait is almost over.

"Work for six months trying to find a publisher and then self-publish," was the advice I received from various sources. That was last November, and when April rolled around, we decided to wait no longer. John helped me research different self-publishing services.

Doug, a fellow Bayliner-owner, wrote to tell me that a friend of his had recently published her book using a service called Createspace, by amazon.com.

There were a few tears and pouting sessions as I submitted files, changed, corrected, and re-submitted. This took a few weeks but finally, the files were deemed acceptable for printing and within hours of requesting a paper proof to be mailed, we received an email that it had been shipped.

I arrive in Barrie, Ontario on April 22nd, and my proof is

scheduled to arrive on April 19th. It works well because shipping the same thing to Roatan would take 2-4 weeks.

Hopefully, the proof looks good, and I won't have to change and resubmit files and order another proof.

Apr 29, 2011

My proof arrived in Barrie a few days before I did, and, after chasing around town, I finally found it at the UPS depot. I should have ordered more than one copy because even after a week of proofing, I know I've missed things.

Martha, who spent several months in Roatan with her husband Doug, came out to visit me in Barrie, and she offered to help me, since she was a professional proof-reader before retiring. I made a round of corrections/revisions, and this time ordered three copies, one for me, one for Martha, and one extra.

Hopefully, we can proofread, make corrections, and still order copies to arrive before I fly back to Roatan. That is one week today so I'm a little stressed but better to get it right and wait a little longer.

I'd rather be writing than self-publishing. It is no fun at all, so let's hope after the first book I can find a publisher for the next one.

I am enjoying my visit with my family and getting to know Kendra and Jordana, my two granddaughters. I wish I could bottle some of this fresh, cool Canadian air to take back to Roatan with me because summer is steamy there!

May 27, 2011

Steamy, sticky, and smoky weather is what I returned to. The temperature reads 88 degrees, but the heat index that the weatherman quotes, makes it feel like 100.

At first, I chalked the smoky air up to the burning of vegetation on the mainland being carried across to the island by the prevailing winds. Then someone told me that a volcano in Nicaragua has been spewing ash for the past month and sending it our way. They call it vog.

Martha did a great job of proofreading for me. I took the proof and five pages of notes containing 149 changes/corrections to the courier and shipped it to Clearwater, Florida. Marcia, another of my island friends, was visiting her mother there. The package was scheduled to arrive on Friday, May 20th. Marcia was leaving Clearwater around 2-3 pm to drive to Miami on Monday, May 23rd to catch an early Tuesday flight.

The tracking information showed a delay at US customs, and the delivery was rescheduled for an end of the day Monday. Thankfully, Marcia waited for the delivery before leaving for Miami and I was sitting at the airport in Roatan waiting for her when her plane landed on Tuesday morning.

After making the 149 changes, which took about 4 hours of uninterrupted work, I gave some thought to my cover, which I really hadn't liked since seeing the first proof. Martha had given me her honest impression of the cover, and I knew deep down that she was right. It stunk!

The self-publishing program includes a "cover creator", which lets me choose from several designs but doesn't allow for much flexibility within each design. So, I went back to the drawing board and spent a couple of days trying to find a better design, which I believe I have done.

The photos in the proof were fuzzy, so solving the issue of the low-resolution photos was the next task at hand. This has been baffling me for weeks. My jpeg resizer program allowed me to increase the resolution to 300 dpi on all my photos, but as soon as I convert the word document to a PDF file the photos revert to their original resolution. I found advice on google and clicked off a default setting on my Adobe program. This seemed to correct the problem. I submitted a new PDF file for review and did not receive a nasty message about low-resolution photos.

Because Amazon is an American company and I am a Canadian citizen, I had to file for a US taxpayer ID number. This I did by filing a W-7 form (downloaded from the internet), along with a letter from Amazon stating that they are acting as a withholding agent for me and a copy of my passport photo which we had to

have notarized by our lawyer here on the island.
Once I receive my US taxpayer ID, I then must file a W-8BEN form, on which the number will be entered. This will prevent Amazon from withholding 30% of my royalties for taxes. Canada has a non-withholding treaty with the US, but the paperwork must be filed.

Once again, we turned to island friends returning to civilization to send our mail. This time, it was Cindy and Troy Beasley, who flew back last week and agreed to mail my letter to the IRS from the States.

My next challenge is to order the third, and hopefully, final proof and have it sent to Chuck, who has his sailboat docked in front of *Diamond Lil* here at the Point. Chuck is flying to the island from California on June 2nd. I was aiming for May 27th as the date to order the proof, so he would receive it in time and that is today!

John, walking along the sidewalk along the south shore of The Point

New Year's Day gathering at The Crow's Nest, Marble Hill Farms

Towing *El Tanko* behind us, on the way to Port Royal

Diamond Lil, on a mooring ball by the Cow and Calf in Port Royal

The collection of boats tied to *Free Radical,* in Port Royal

Lisa and Betty, finally in Roatan after a brief stop in Belize

Chapter 11

June 18, 2011

The wait is over! The Captain's Log - Diamond Lil Does the Loop is now available on amazon.com

The marketing stage begins now. I shipped a book to several magazine publishers whom I've worked with, in the past, and hope to have some of them print a review in their magazine.

I also shipped a copy to the Executive Director of America's Great Loop Cruisers' Association (AGLCA), Janice Kromer, whom I have also corresponded with in the past, hoping that she can recommend the book to her members, of which there are hundreds.

I began working on book #2 this week, despite our busy social calendar. Each morning I stroll along the dock, past our tropical plants, climb the five steps up into the house, hang a left, along a narrow hallway, my bare feet slapping against the faded, terra cotta tile floor, into the great room, which I am fortunate enough to use as my office.

The entire side of the room facing the boat, where John sits while I work, is made up of doors and shutters that open up, so we can see each other, from a distance.

I sit at the table, facing the wide, shaded balcony, with the same cool, faded terra cotta tile floor. Across the bay, I have a view of the candy-colored houses of Pandy

Town, built on stilts over the water, against the background of lush, tropical mountains. To my right is the Caribbean Sea, stunning no matter what her mood.

To the left, lies the small channel that connects five or six small towns and neighborhoods. Some call it Water World, or Little Venice. It's the highway of life here, and there is no lack of action to watch when my eyes and brain need a break from my work.

Day by day, The Captain's Log - Diamond Lil Does the Bahamas, slowly comes to life. I retrieve my VCR and television set out of their hiding spot and set them up each day, fast forward my video to the part I'm writing about and watch. I read my log. I read the six cruising guides that I am using, and I pour over the charts, re-tracing every route through every cut that we navigated. I want to make sure to get every detail right. When I'm unsure, I check with my right-hand man, the captain.

As the noon hour approaches, John will yell out from the boat.

"MEL --- LUNCH"

I'm sure everyone who hears, and they do because sound travels easily across the water, must find us an odd pair, as I bounce along the dock and climb on board to see what delicious meal he has in store for me.

"John, remember that day that we were dragged

through the anchorage in Marsh Harbour, by that big powerboat, *The Judge's Choice*?" I asked him, yesterday.

"Did we have two anchors down that day or just our Danforth?"

"We had two down, because it was so crowded, and we didn't want to swing too much," he replied.

"I thought so, that's what I wrote, but I wanted to check to make sure."

And so it goes, day by day, week by week. My daily goal is to write 1,500 words.

October 27, 2011

If you could lift your house, swing it around 180 degrees, and set it back down, facing the opposite direction, even if just for a few days, for a change, would you?

One of the joys of living on a boat is the ability to do just that. When Hurricane Rina was described on CNN as "bearing down on Honduras," John scratched his chin and gazed off into space.

"I think we should turn the boat around, at the very least. All the wind is going to come from the west and the north. We would be really sorry if something happened."

Anxiety washed over me as I tried to envision the plan.

"Can we at least wait until Joe, Doug, and LH get back from down island?" I pleaded. "We sure could use the help."

Patches of rain, driven sideways along the canal by the wicked wind of the west, etched random patterns on the surface of the water. Lines creaked and moaned, as horrific images of attempting to maneuver the boat in howling wind raced through my troubled mind.

"We need to do it before dark. It's easy," assured the captain, still scratching at the two-day, pre-hurricane stubble on his chin.

"We don't even need to start the engines. We will just tie the bow off, push the stern out, and the wind will do the rest."

"But how will we get the stern back in once it swings around?" I asked, unable to envision the sequence of events. I vaguely remembered doing this back home, years ago, in our narrow canal in Keswick, but here, in the tropical storm wind, along a busy waterway, it seemed a much more daunting task.

"Don't worry. You'll see," he said. "Climb up on the bow and cleat the end of this line off on the port side."

I wound the long, back-up anchor line under the pair of anchors that hang on the pulpit, cleated it off, hopped back down, and helped the captain switch fenders from the starboard to the port side.

I stood on the dock by the bow, with the long anchor line in my hand, while John pushed the stern of the boat out into the canal for the wind to work its magic. I guided the bow so it didn't scrape along the dock and eased it along the dock as the stern came slowly around to rest on the opposite side, precisely the way John had promised me it would.

We disassembled our power cord, neatly arranged along the length of the dock, tucked in and under trees and shrubs, and re-positioned it, across the lawn between the dock and the house, in order that it would reach across the aft deck to the starboard side, which is where the connections on the boat are.

We are docked on the "wrong" side of the boat now, as our water intake is also on the starboard side, but these are minor details. We are positioned with our bow into the gusting wind and are ready for Tropical Storm Rina.

Inside the boat, we barely feel the wind. Our back door, which we have had closed against the driving rain for the past week, can be left wide open. Even our port side windows, facing south, are open and dry behind me, as I face the streams of rain rolling down the outside of the windows across from me.

Despite the oncoming hurricane, I am giddy with excitement. Everything seems as new to me as if we'd taken a trip. Instead of facing the house and my growing collection of tropical plants, as I have for the past two and a half years, I face the canal.

Twin shrimp boats, with enormous green nets hanging above their decks, are docked on the other side. There is a flurry of activity aboard both ships.

Along the avenue, which is what they call the narrow little road through town, I see the row of *tiendas* or small grocery stores. Directly across from us is Hessie's, a two-story concrete structure, painted golden yellow with white trim and a covered balcony on the second floor.

To the left of Hessie's is the shrimp factory, where scores of employees pour out onto the dock at break time, identically shod in squeaky clean, sparkling white, rubber boots.

When I turn my head to the right, which normally is to the west, and the little footbridge that connects our spit of land to the town of Oak Ridge, I now face east, and my view is of the candy-colored houses, perched on stilts above the water, that dot the shoreline, and behind the houses, the majestic peaks of Pandy Town, one of the most stunning, backdrops on the entire island.

I left John to finish tying lines while I ducked out to capture a shot of the twin shrimp boats. Tiny raindrops set the mood in front of an ominous, orange sky. Thankful later to have captured the moment in time, I woke in the middle of the night and looked out across the water, to find them gone, in search of somewhere safer to ride out the storm.

Early to bed, we went, not sure what to expect during the night, and we had company. I had first spotted him

203

as I lay reading in bed the night before. A mouse, I thought, at first, as he ran along beside my bed, and disappeared behind John's closet.

I flung my book in one direction, my reading glasses in another, vaulted from the bed and rushed through the boat, scaring the hell out of John, who sat peacefully at the captain's table, with his headphones on, playing his favorite video game.

Pausing his game, John went in to save the day, a long knife in one hand, a flashlight in the other - in search of the creature, but it was gone, or so it seemed. The volume of the chewing sound above our heads a few hours later led me to believe that it was more likely a rat than a mouse, but either way, eventually we slept and woke in the morning, thankful to find that we had dodged the bullet.

The storm had moved far enough to the north that we would experience nothing more than the heavy rain and driving wind that has been with us all week. A little cabin fever, to be sure, but on the bright side, a brand-new vista. So, if you could, with little effort, even for just a few days, swing your house around 180 degrees, would you?

Nov 21, 2011

"I can't live with these rats any longer," I wailed. "*La Feets* is overrun with them and now they're beginning to come into the boat."

The little shed which was named *La Feets* was where the bags of dog kibble were stored. Joe had tried putting the bags in a large cooler, to keep the rats out, but they chewed through it. I had suggested a metal container, but so far nothing had come of it.

When it was time to feed the dogs or do laundry and I open the door to *La Feets* and flicked on the light, an increasing number of the ugly rodents scurried off into the dark corners. John was as creeped out as I was.

Joe had left poison, but we didn't like to use it. Our neighbors had pets. and we were afraid of them being poisoned. We tried setting traps and rigging up pails of water with some tempting food on a stick stretched over the water. Nothing had worked.

"Alana has kittens she wants to find homes for. She texted me this morning with a picture of a cute black and white one. I really think that is our solution. I know you didn't want a cat on the boat, but if we go away for a while, I'm sure we can leave her here with whoever is watching the property," I pleaded.

"We'll see," said the captain, as he looked up from his book. It wasn't a no, so I decided to be patient. Not easy for me.

Nov 22, 2011

"Come on, woman. Let's go get your critter."

Nothing had been said about the cat I wanted since I mentioned it.

"Really? Cool!," I beamed as I scrambled to call Alana and tell her the good news. We were coming up to the farm to get our new cat. One of the things we had missed during these years of cruising was having a pet.

"What are you going to name her?" John asked, several hours later, after we had returned to the boat with our new boat kitty.

"I will ask her," I said. "What is your name?"

"Minut," she mewed, or so it sounded to me.

"Minut", I said, pronounced Minew. It did not occur to me, at the time, that it was French for cat. Subliminally, I suppose my Canadian upbringing had implanted it in my brain.

"I didn't hear that," said John. "Whatever. It's your critter."

Nov 23, 2011

Even in Paradise, there is work to be done.

Diamond Lil requires a lot of attention if she is to be kept looking at her best at this point in her life. It's a harsh climate for an old girl, to say the least.

We haven't returned *DL* to her usual position on the dock. First, John wants to finish the work he is doing on our radar arch up in the flybridge.

Once we do swing back around, the afternoon, or evening sun, as they would say here, is hot on the back of the boat, and we cannot sit out there. Even the inside of the boat heats up this time of day, so we asked our friend Julie, who does canvas work, to fashion us a sunscreen for the aft deck, so we could snap it down in the evening and roll it up in the morning or when we travel. Julie did an excellent job, and the new addition looks great.

The next job was the reupholstering of the headliner that goes around the sides and top of our bed. The stained and tattered, 24-year-old material was ripped off the form. Luckily, the veranda on the big house is large enough to spread the 16-foot long piece out on the floor. John and I worked together, recovering the form with new material that we found in French Harbour, at a little *taperia* (sewing store) called Valdina's.

Dec 25, 2011

Miss Lisa returned to the island for the holidays, staying with us for three weeks this time. After accepting invitations from friends and neighbors for Christmas dinner over the last few years, we decided that this year it was our turn to host the Christmas party. Our friend, Janet, from Australia, summed it up in an email message I received the next morning.

"I cannot believe I am still eating as I ate for hours at

the Christmas Party across the bay at the end of the
Point. Mel and John were great hosts; she cooked
pumpkin, cherry, and Key Lime pies and they were
excellent with perfectly flaky crusts and the filling
cooked exactly right. John stuffed and roasted the
turkey and it was very juicy and full of flavor; turkey is
not my favorite but this one was so good I had two
helpings.

Actually, I had two to three helpings of everything,
determined to not be outdone. This was a bring a plate
deal as we say in OZ - just remembered that the Yanks
say "potluck" - and there was way too much food - so I
did my best. First, there were TWO bowls of mashed
potatoes (first thing I noticed pretending to glance only
casually at the table laden beyond its designed load), a
huge and delicious Caesar salad, stuffing hot and
steaming and smelling buttery and herby, a HUGE jug
of gravy (no lumps!), cranberries, a jalapeno quiche,
crab dip, Virginia Ham and a pasta seafood salad - and
fresh-baked bread. Now I want to tell you it was a real
challenge getting some of everything on my plate, but I
approached this much like hanging up a full basket of
washing in a small area - it took creativity and
organization, but I got there in the end even managing
to carry this high pile of food back to my chair with no
spillage - not even a drop of the gravy which smothered
everything, but the salad was lost.

I sat with Betty and Joe and bite by bite worked my way
from the outside in - this was to avoid spilling one
crumb .... then we were joined by BJ and Tracy (Cap'n
Ed watched the cafe) and I said "You know; I think I
could eat some more ....." so up I went for more turkey,
potatoes, gravy, and salad - I did hold back - I do have
manners .....

Then I strolled outside for a short walk so as to be fresh

for the deserts - we had all of Mel's pies plus my Cherry Cobbler and an enormous bowl of fruit salad and another bowl of Waldorf Salad. I am proud to say that once again I managed to put some of everything on my plate and ate it all and then went back up to the table to tidy up some of the ragged edges that some people had so crassly left on the pies. I mean, really, where are their manners?

As you can imagine by this point I thought what the hell - why hold back - and went back for just one more hit of cherry pie - but some bloody woman got there before me and finished it off which kind of pissed me off, so I had to settle for my own Cherry Cobbler .... whew, how boring.

OK; now we have a big problem because the return trip to BJ's was by dinghy and getting into that little bugger was a bitch before I ate. I managed to waddle down the dock and was not too proud to ask Joe and Betty to help me into the boat, and then with getting out of it at BJ's.

Like many people who visit, Lisa fell in love with Roatan and couldn't wait to return. Her first visit was this past February, and now, before the year was even out, she is back!

The week she spent here the first time just wasn't long enough. This time, she managed to get three weeks away from the office and arrived on Dec 17th. We hurried from the airport to Oak Ridge, where the wrapping party for the children of Calabash/Fiddler's Bight Christmas party was underway, at BJs Backyard BBQ. We ordered Lisa a cold Salva Vida and put her to work wrapping gifts.

A few days later, we put Lisa to work once again, this time at the kids' party. Her first task was to hand out fluorescent bracelets to the girls and help them to put them on. Later, she was given the task of handing out gifts to the "older girls." Some of these kids can be a little pushy, but we chose the right woman for the job.

Lisa was a good "Santa" herself, arriving on the island with lots of goodies. 2012 calendars, magazines for the girls, Tetley tea for the admiral, and cigars for the captain, were just a few of her offerings.

We enjoyed a couple of trips down island to attempt some Christmas shopping and Lisa received a first-hand experience with the daunting task of hunting down elusive items on the island. By the time she left, she knew where all the good stores were, and what order we needed to shop them, to have the most success.

Speaking of elusive items, we were hoping for turnip with our Christmas meal and searched every grocery store and vegetable stand between Coxen Hole and Oak Ridge, but found not a single turnip. The captain went out a few days later, despite his intense hatred of turnip, and also came up empty-handed.

Our Christmas dinner, shared with 28 neighbors and friends, was a great success, despite the lack of turnip, and I was very thankful to have Lisa's help.

Lisa had a chance to meet more of our friends and we enjoyed visiting all our local hot spots. We ventured east to La Sirena de Camp Bay, also known as "Asylum," but mostly referred to as "Jimmy's place," up in Camp Bay, almost as far east as the road goes, with "road" being a loose term.

The three weeks flew by and before long, it was time to make the return trip to the airport, not nearly as exciting as the trip down, three weeks before, but it warmed my heart when Lisa told me that she had "the best vacation of her life."

Removing old material and stuffing from the headliner on our bed

The newly reupholstered headliner, back in the master stateroom

Minut, the first day we brought her home to the boat

The colorful stilt houses of Panty Town, Roatan

Proofreading my second book, Diamond Lil Does the Bahamas

An ominous sky the night before TS Rina

John and Julie, fitting the sunscreen to the transom on *Diamond Lil*

Our new sunscreen to protect us from the harsh afternoon sun

Chapter 12

Jan 21, 2012

Outside the big house on the Point, the wind is howling. Whitecaps race across the bay and palm trees are bent over in the wind. John is in the kitchen, preparing dinner. Mom Wood is out on the verandah, enjoying the rush hour traffic on our little waterway. Dad is lying on the couch in the living room, book in hand. Minut is curled up between his legs, as she has been much of the time he's been here.

I am sitting at the dining room table, which is normally my desk, where I write. However, tonight it is a dining room table. I have my laptop in front of me and am getting messages from several of our friends. They know that Mom and Dad are catching the cruise ship in Roatan tomorrow, to head back to Florida. That is if the cruise ship can make it into Mahogany Bay.

Roatan is working on improving the cruise ship facility. Currently, docking in high winds is often impossible. On several occasions, friends of ours who were expecting friends from a cruise ship had been disappointed when high winds prevented the ship from stopping in Roatan.

It is their last night of a two-week stay with us here on the island. They visited once in the past, by cruise ship, but only for a day. We gave them a whirlwind island tour that day, as we had to return them to the ship by 4:00 pm.

"This wind is forecast to pick up," I announce, looking up from my laptop. "Several of our friends have written to warn us that the ship may not come in tomorrow morning, after all."

"They know that we are here and have promised to come for us," Dad attempted to reassure me.

Roatan is one of the most popular Western Caribbean cruise ship destinations. When Mom and Dad discovered that they could cruise from Tampa, Florida to Roatan on Holland America's ms Rotterdam, visit for a couple of weeks, and then cruise back to Florida, they jumped at the chance. It sounded like a great way to escape the rat race of airports and the confines of an airplane. With Mom being mobility challenged, they had enjoyed numerous cruises in the past.

The other advantage of coming to the island by cruise ship is the ability to bring more and larger items than when flying. Mom and Dad came loaded with goodies, including a new generator for *Diamond Lil*, so that we can do more cruising, a new battery charger, Advantage pest control for Minut, a file of 650 books for our Kindles, and a whole carton of Canadian rye whiskey.

We had agreed to pick them up at 10:00 am at the Mahogany Bay Cruise Ship terminal. Partway along the long road leading into the terminal, we were shocked to see Dad, standing at the side of the road, with a young black man holding his bag.

"You're two hours late," Dad told us as we pulled up.

"It's not quite ten," said John.

"That's ship's time," said Dad. Or 8:00 am, Roatan time."

"Oh, sorry," we said at the same time, mortified that they had been there for two hours.

"Well, it's ok," said Dad. "Mr. Dog Bite here has taken good care of me."

"When he said he was coming to see his son, John, on Oak Ridge Point," said Dog Bite, "I knew he meant you."

John had hired Dog Bite, who does have a real name, one which I don't remember, to do some work on *El Tanko*, Joe's skiff that we use to get around by water. Joe's dog, Chiquita, had given him a nasty bite on the leg.

"I told you that dog bites," he said after John paid for his medical care. John nicknamed him Dog Bite. It seemed to be that he loved the name, for that is how he had introduced himself to John's Dad.

We loaded Dad into the car and went to the terminal to retrieve Mom, who was waiting patiently for us, and headed back to Oak Ridge.

Mom and Dad were greeted warmly by our large group of friends. We showed them many of our favorite spots on the island. Several visitors dropped by to meet the folks and enjoy a cold beverage and a chat on the shady front porch of the big house.

Miss Jessie and Eulina sent over home-made bread. Starvin Marvin stopped by with fresh lobster. Mark dropped off three ripe pineapples. Benut's Mom, Miss Anna, from Pandy Town, sent over homemade coconut candy.

"This is grocery shopping, island-style," I told them, as we dug into our fresh, home-made and home-caught goodies.

Jan 22, 2012

Morning brought no respite from the howling wind. The word was that Mom and Dad's ship would not be able to get in the channel but would bypass our little island.

Roatan Joe was due to arrive in a few days, bringing a few friends with him for a couple of weeks. He had generously offered the house for Mom and Dad to stay in. However, with him arriving soon, we would have to find somewhere else for them to stay if they didn't catch the cruise ship.

"Luckily, they got packed last night," said John, as I moaned and groaned, wondering what on earth we would do.

"Hurry up and get dressed. We'll run down to the airport and see if there are any flights going to Florida."

We loaded the folks and their luggage into *El Tanko* and set off for BJs. We packed them into Joe's little red Toyota and had our friend, Doug, meet us with his pickup truck for their luggage. The car was too small for them and the luggage. Off we headed, down the island, with Doug following.

We passed the Mahogany Bay Cruise ship terminal, which is just this side of the airport and alas, there was no ship in sight.

"What about the other terminal?" Dad asked. "The one in Coxen Hole. Maybe there is a ship there we can get on. Let's check before we go to the airport."

"That is doubtful, Dad," said John, trying to keep his cool. "We could miss a flight to Florida in the meantime."

"Well, let's check," insisted Dad.

We snaked our way through downtown Coxen Hole, never an easy feat, and arrived outside the busy cruise ship terminal. Dad and I jumped out and headed for the gate.

"Can I get on this ship?" Dad blurted out to the gatekeeper.

The man fired back an answer in rapid Spanish.

"We should ask where the ship is going, Dad. Maybe it isn't heading for Florida."

I asked, in my best, but not great Spanish, if the ship was headed for Florida and if there was any way my dad could get on it, knowing as I asked that it wasn't going to happen.

"Si, si," replied the man, followed by another couple of sentences in rapid Spanish.

"What did he say?" asked Dad. "It sounded like he said yes."

He said that the ship is going to Florida. He said no to you getting on it. You can only buy the tickets in Florida, before the cruise leaves port.

Off we went, back to the airport, once again with Doug following behind in his pickup truck.

John, who doesn't smoke in front of his parents and had been hiding his habit for two weeks, paced outside the airport, while Doug and I attempted to get Mom and Dad on a flight home. There were no flights to Tampa.

There were two seats, however, on a flight to Miami. From there, they could catch another flight, to Tampa.

I really felt for Mom, who had mobility issues, taking two flights instead of a comfortable cruise ship, but there wasn't much choice. They had to fly from Roatan to Houston. Due to the storm, they missed their connection to Tampa and had to overnight in Houston. Their luggage made it to Tampa, however, so they were stuck in Houston with nothing but the clothes on their backs.

When I asked about their night in Houston, Dad told me that they were woken the next morning, in the hotel recommended by the airport, by the barking of dogs from a kennel, situated about 10 feet from their room.

Feb 13, 2012

An electric head, commonly known as a toilet, had been on our wish list for a long time. We were longing to replace the hand-pump model that came with the boat. In fact, two hand-pump toilets were on the boat when we bought her. We needed storage for the captain's tools more than we needed a second head, so we converted our powder room to a tool room.

Our new electric head was a Christmas gift from Mom and Dad Wood. John spent countless hours on the internet, researching different models and shopping for the best price. As usual, he found the item, and then I placed the order. We began the inevitable, long wait to have it shipped to the island.

Four weeks passed. Just when we thought our new head would arrive, John noticed that the money for it had been refunded to our Visa account. OH NO!

We had no choice but to re-order, this time from another source. By the time the head arrived on our island, it was Feb 9th. Joe was due to arrive on Feb 12th.

The plan had been to use the washroom in the house while John installed the new head. It didn't quite work out that way, but Joe was very understanding as we wandered in and out of his house to use his washroom for a couple of days.

We had replaced the other walls in the room when we did our shower repair. We had put off replacing the final wall until our electric head arrived.

Every inch of the boat was covered with tools, pipes, and wire. I picked up countless bits and pieces that appeared to me to be scraps of garbage. When I tried to throw them out, John insisted that no, they are priceless bits and pieces, coveted items, which we must save for a rainy day. Into the junk drawer, they must go, along with the countless other unrecognizable scraps of man-junk.

Finally, after two days of work, feeding wires through walls and changing plumbing, which runs under the floor of the boat and requires that the captain works on his hands and knees, we were ready for a test run.

Clean water was used, of course, for this trial, and it was a good thing, for when John pushed the nifty little button on the wall, the water was not flushed down the drain, but flung back at us. It was a LOT of water.

Back to the drawing board, he went. The new head came back out. John hauled it outside, hooked it up to a battery, and ran the hose into it. FLUSH! Down the water went, instead of coming back at us. It is the plumbing that's the problem, not the head itself, we realized.

Meanwhile, the old toilet was left, ugly and embarrassing, outside on the dock, for the duration. I begged John to drag it to the garbage pick-up spot, but he insisted that we keep it, just in case the new one didn't work out. This thought tortured me. There is no way that ugly old, creaky, cracked, leaky head was coming back on board this boat!

Hindsight is 20/20. We should have changed all the plumbing when we installed the new head. Back down on my knees, I went, on the undersized galley floor, while John went back down on his knees in the *bano*, his legs twisted uncomfortably in the tiny space. We finally managed to remove the old sewage hose, not a pleasant task. Then, we fed the new hose through the cramped space under the floor of the boat and reconnected it.

Three days later, the job was done. The tools were put away, the mess cleaned up, and the final photos were taken of our HEAD JOB FROM HELL!

March 8, 2012

"The good, the bad and the ugly; that's what people like to read about." Those were the words of advice that I received years ago, from Natalie, editor of PassageMaker magazine.

We were discussing article ideas for an upcoming submission to their magazine.

"With the emphasis on the ugly," she added.
I try to keep her advice in mind as I write because it turned out that she was right. Our website readers

enjoy following our life in the sunny south. However, when something bad happens, like a hurricane or a coup, a riot or an earthquake, the daily hits on our website go through the roof. Yes, Natalie, people love the ugly.

Add a pirate to the recipe, add water, and stir. The very word "pirate" demands attention. A pirate is a thief at sea. They're everywhere on land -muggers, robbers, and thieves, but only when they pillage from those who choose to live on the water can they call themselves pirates. I've borrowed other boaters' pirates over the years. We've visited remote spots with buddy boats at times, taken turns keeping watch all night, guarding against pirates. But so far, after six years of living and traveling on *Diamond Lil*, we haven't had first-hand experience with a pirate, until this past week.

The captain is normally up before me in the morning. Thursday morning was no different. He gets up, brushes his teeth, reaches for his kindle, and heads upstairs, where he reads, quietly, until I get up. If I sleep long enough, I hear him come down to the galley, take the kettle off the stove, go out to the back deck, fill it with water, and put it on the stove to boil. The fan above my bed slows as the power supply dips, so even if I don't hear this, I sense it, and it wakes me up. That's fine because it's coffee time, and there is no better coffee than Honduran coffee.

On this particular morning, I stumbled out of our bedroom, properly referred to as the "main cabin," after brushing my own teeth. As I stepped past the spare bedroom or guest cabin, I noticed my purse on the floor, with a little baggie full of business cards scattered about.

That wasn't there when I went to bed, I thought. That damn pregnant cat has been rummaging around in here. Then I noticed a new shirt, pulled from the hanger in my closet, or storage locker, also lying on the floor. Not really a cat kind of a mess. Picking up my purse and stuffing the little baggie full of business cards back in, I instinctively reached for my wallet, which was not where it should be, nor in either of the other two sections of my purse.

"Honey, do you see my wallet out there? It's not in my purse. My purse was on the ground and my wallet is gone. Someone has been in here."

"I'm sure it's here somewhere. Nobody has been in here," said hubby.

"Do you have your laptop?" I asked.

"No. I've just been reading," he answered.

"Where was it, when you went to bed?" I asked. By this time, he was by my side.

"Right there," he said, pointing to an empty spot on the bed, right beside my laptop, which luckily, was still there. And then I knew. No laptop. No wallet.

I hung the pink shirt back up and reached down, under all the clothes. That is where I hide my external hard drive. Each day, after I've finished writing, I back up my book. It too was gone.

Where had my camera been, I wondered? It was in my purse when we went out the day before. It was gone. John's cell phone too was gone - unplugged from the charger that it had been plugged into when he went to bed.

Footprints on the swim platform led us to believe that we had been visited by pirates, versus the everyday thieves who come by land. As the day went by, we discovered more and more items missing. Several flashlights, a Tigo internet stick, and John's Crocs, which Lisa had brought from Canada, were all gone.

"Wait a minute," John said. "That's who did it‑ the shoe thief."

About a year ago, an identical pair of Crocs, also from Canada, had gone missing from our aft deck one night while we slept. At the time, I insisted that someone had been on the aft deck of our boat and stolen them. The captain refused to accept this possibility, back then, but he does now. He believes that this shoe thief enjoyed the first pair of Crocs so much that he came back for a new pair, once they wore out. Only this time, the shoe thief wondered what else might be lying around that he might like, or like to sell, or trade for crack cocaine, perhaps!

"Shoe pirate," I reminded John

"Whatever."

So now, we've lost our innocence and sleep with our back door locked tight, hot as that is on an eighty‑five‑degree night in the tropics. John will get a good chain, like in apartment buildings back in the real world, and we'll have the door open, wide enough for a cat, but not wide enough for pirates.

All we need to do is watch for a guy wearing black Crocs from Canada.

April 11, 2012

About a month ago, as I was walking towards the boat, I caught a flash of movement up on our flybridge. Upon scaling our ladder, I discovered a large, orange cat, crouching down in the space under the dashboard. My first thought was that it was a male cat, sniffing around our as yet un-spayed Minut.

As I bent down towards the cat, it flew past me, leaped down from the flybridge and scurried off. A couple of days later, I saw the cat again. This time, I got a closer look. It was no male cat. It was a very pregnant female cat.

"The poor thing," I moaned. "We can't just get rid of it. We'll wait until it has it's kittens and then find homes for them all."

"I agreed to ONE cat," John argued. "How do you expect to find a home for kittens and a mother cat?"

"I will," I promised, wondering how the hell I was going to manage that.

When I asked John what he wanted to name the cat, he said, "Gone." I named her Mucho because she eats a lot. The cat never seems to get enough to eat.

Last night, Mucho flopped down inside the guest cabin, panting and heaving. She proceeded to produce three identical orange kittens. After a short delay, the fourth kitten was born – also an identical orange one. It looks like I have some work to do to find homes for them all. There isn't room on this ship for six cats!

May 12, 2012

I love to visit Alana at her farm, just up the hill from Oak Ridge. We had been to visit once, about a month ago. There were four foals, two colts, and two fillies, frolicking around the pasture. They had all been born within a couple of weeks of each other, while I was in Canada visiting my family.

Yesterday, we stopped in to visit Alana once again.

"I want to keep Fiona, the bay filly," said Alana. "One of the colts is spoken for," she said, over our frosty Salva Vidas.

"I have so many horses to feed already," she continued. I really must get rid of the other two foals."

"Do you want one?" asked John, out of the blue.

I almost fell off the picnic table in shock. I had a pony and a horse when I was young. I hadn't remotely considered the possibility of having another one at this point in my life.

"What? Where would we keep a horse? We live on a boat."

"You could board it here," said Alana. I would only charge you enough to cover the feed."

"Wow. Well, I don't know if we can afford it," I answered. "What would you charge us for one?"

"How about 1,000 lempiras?" she answered. "Say 500 lempiras a month for the board."

I have never seen John reach for his wallet so quickly. She had that 1,000 lempiras ($50.00) plus the first month's board ($25.00) in her hand before I knew it.

I had two foals to choose from. We walked out to the pasture and watched them trotting towards us. The little buckskin filly trotted as if she was floating. It gave me goosebumps to watch her move.

"That one," I said.

"That's Morena," said Alana.

And just like that, I, who live on a boat, and at the ripe, old age of 55, have a two-month-old horse! I feel like a kid on Christmas morning. I keep pinching myself to make sure it's not a dream. We keep putting more and more roots down here. I am beginning to think we will never leave Roatan.

May 25, 2012

Blue, green, yellow, and pink are the names of the four kittens that were born six weeks ago. Believe it or not, I found a home for Mucho and three of the kittens.

RB, from Marble Hill, wanted a male. So did our friend, Kim, from Port Royal. Kim rushed over and chose hers. We painted the nails on all four paws yellow. I painted the nails on the only other male kitten blue, for RB. She named him Ruffy, and he is going to live in Diamond Rock.

That left pink and green, who we named Poncho and Lefty. The manager from Barbareta, a privately owned island to the east of us, which is part of Roatan, but separated by water, took Lefty. Our friends at Royal

Playa Resort took Mucho, the mother cat, to solve their rodent issues. They renamed her "Pretty."

That left Poncho. She was an odd duck, with a habit of staring off into space with her mouth hanging just slightly open, looking somewhat "not complete" as they refer to mentally handicapped people here on the island. A friend inquired about Poncho. She knew a nun in Coxen Hole who wanted a cat. John, who had been so adamant about only having only one cat, agreed with me that Coxen Hole was no place for our slightly incomplete Poncho.

That makes four of us now, living on *Diamond Lil* — John, me, Minut, and Poncho. We are beginning our own Noah's Ark collection.

Mom and Dad Wood, enjoying the Friday fun at BJs Backyard

Janet, joining the Banditos at BJs Backyard

John and Dad, taking in the sights of Oak Ridge Harbour

Mom, enjoying the boat ride.

Morena, at 2 months of age when we bought her

John, sharing the space on *Diamond Lil* with two of the kittens

Chapter 13

Aug 19, 2012

It's been a year and two months since I published my first book - The Captain's Log - Diamond Lil Does the Loop.

When John and I returned to Roatan from our summer trip to Canada, I dug out my Bahamas logs, photos, and videotapes and began work on book #2. This one is called The Captain's Log - Diamond Lil Does the Bahamas.

I worked religiously, from Monday to Friday and half a day each Saturday, week after week, trying to bring our Bahamas adventures to life in the form of this book. Because it is the off-season or summer, many of our friends have gone north for six months. With fewer social obligations, it is easier to stay with the work.

"MEL - LUNCH!" I heard each day around noon, as I had while I wrote the first book. After all this time, it still made me chuckle, for in Roatan, it is mostly the women who do the cooking, calling the men in for lunch. Sound carries across the water, and I'm sure the fishermen and townsfolk think that a man calling his wife in for lunch is strange.

Once again, as I had the previous year, I went back to work after lunch, usually, until I heard the telltale sound of John dumping a bucketful of ice from our ice maker into the cooler we keep out on our aft deck. This sound meant that the captain was getting ready for the happy hour. My reward for reaching my daily goal of 1,500 words, once again, was a frosty *Salva Vida*.

Slowly but surely, the second book took shape. The proofreading began, with first Lori Soule and then Joe Berta taking a crack at it. Each time I went through the book, from start to finish, making the changes and corrections that these two supportive friends sent me.

One day I was sitting with another friend, Marcia Quinn, a retired writer and editor. "I don't know why you don't let me proofread it," she commented.

Thus began my first experience with working with an editor, a humbling experience. I had to chuckle when John and I sat with Marcia and her husband Dennis at Cal's one evening.

"You DO know the rules of comma use, don't you?" she asked me, quite tactfully.

"I guess not," I had to admit, for I realized that this was one of my weaknesses. Grade school punctuation lessons are a distant memory for me.

So began my third re-write. Many, many commas came out, and a few were added. My compound words also took a beating - one word, two words, a hyphen, no hyphen - it was another lesson learned.

"YIKES - long sentence" - she would write, "You don't need to make your readers work so hard," alongside the bright yellow markings on my digital draft. She was correct, of course, and I went back through the book and attempted to correct these long, run-on sentences.

I was desperate to finish the book before John and I flew back to Canada for our summer visit, but this did not happen. I worked on the book at Lisa's while she was at work. I worked at Suzanne's, with children and grandchildren surrounding me. I worked at Dave's house in Aurora. I worked at three different libraries. One day, I realized that I had lost many of my word documents, including the book.

After briefly considering plunging to my death from Lisa's 8th-floor balcony, I talked on the phone to John, who was back in Roatan. As usual, he talked me through my crisis, and I set to work attempting to recover my lost files.

I had no luck, so my good friend Lori tried for me. She spent several days at this, but in the end, we had un-editable files. Rick Davidson suggested a couple of downloads, but again, I had no success. My son Donald tried. When he threw his hands up in the air, I knew I was beaten. I had no choice but to begin the laborious task of re-doing all the changes to a version that I had from about two weeks earlier.

At this point, Rick offered to proofread my draft. His sharp eyes caught another dozen or so errors. Once I made all these changes, Lori proofread the entire thing for me AGAIN and once again, I made several changes and corrections.

Finally, I had a printable file. I ordered two sets of paper proofs and several digital proofs.

This morning, at 6:48 am, I clicked the button on the *CreateSpace* book publishing and printing program that made my book go live! The message warns that it could take five to seven days to show up on Amazon's list of books for sale. Last time, this happened within a day, so I sit here, with fingers crossed, waiting to see my book become available.

When I return to Roatan, I will resume work on book #3

- DL Does the Rio Dulce. Hopefully, my missing file will be on the old hard drive that is stored down there. It was on my other hard drive, the one that was stolen when John and I were robbed as we lay sleeping one night. So much for backing up files.

September 27, 2012

It's been a while since we fired up our engines, unplugged, and untied this old boat. In two more days, it's time to move her. It will probably take longer to wind up the power cords and put them away than it will take to move *Diamond Lil* to her new home. That's because we're only moving her about 1/4 mile to the west.

All good things must come to an end. We arrived here at Oak Ridge Point to spend three months making a few repairs. We have been here for three and a half years!

Sticky Harbours is a name that our friend, Brian, was going to use for a book title. If he doesn't, I may, because that's what Roatan has turned out to be for us. We're stuck! We've grown roots, literally.

First came the plants, a few here and there, but they grow so fast, and I missed them when we were traveling by boat, so gradually I added more and more.

Then, Minut, our little black and white cat, came into our lives and chased the pesky rats away. Next came Poncho - a little oxygen-deprived at birth, we think. Then John decided that I should have a horse, which was a dream of mine, and so we bought Morena.

Now, with the plants, two cats, and the horse, we figured the boat was going to get a little crowded, so after our house in Canada sold and the dust settled, we picked up a cute little property here on Oak Ridge Point. I should say, we are attempting to buy this piece of property. Things move slowly on the island, and it isn't quite ours yet. But, what the heck? When it came time to move, we talked to the owner. He had no objection to us moving in before the deal was done. We are about to become squatters. How Honduran is that?

While the owner attempts to light a fire under his lawyer's ass, we've been working like crazy, trying to get our new home ready to move into by the end of the month.

Countless loads of trash, carried in by the sea and dumped in our empty lot for years by the neighbors, needed to be picked up and dragged away, all by boat. We are thankful to our faithful garbage collectors, who hauled away an entire dock load of garbage, week after week. There was even an old toilet that we hauled out of the mangroves.

Our first experience with the Municipal Office in Oak Ridge was, not surprisingly, quite ridiculous. We had been burning scrap wood when the officials stopped by and gave us a stern warning. Get a permit or be fined $5,000 lempiras - $250.00. Wait until it rains, they told us, and then go to the office to buy a fire permit. We waited patiently until enough rain fell to soak the property and went over to the Municipal Office for our permit. The lady wasn't in until after lunch. "Come back at 1:00 pm," they said. "Then you can carry her over to see your property."

Back we went, after lunch, and carried the lady over to the property. I assumed she was checking to see if it was wet enough. She pulled up a lawn chair, sat back, crossing her legs, lit a cigarette, and gazed around, quite relaxed.

"Well, can we get a permit?" I asked once she finished her smoke.

"Oh no, you can't get a permit for The Point. You can't burn here," the lady said.

"Why not? Isn't it wet enough?" I asked.

"Oh no. You can never get a permit to burn on the Point. The fire engines can't get over here."

I don't know why she insisted on coming over to tell me that. I suppose a trip to our property was less boring than her regular tasks.

"The only thing you might do," she said, "is to have a fire very late one night when nobody is in the office to answer the phone if someone calls to complain. If it's Sunday night, that could be even better."

Any bonfires we had, from that point on, were on Sunday night, and even then, only when the wind was from the right direction and not too strong.

We were able to get town water hooked up this week. It runs Monday, Wednesday, Friday, and Saturday, between the hours of 8:00 am until 11:00 am.

Eventually, we'll do what everyone else does and put in water storage units. Until then, I'm happy to have water for my plants and to fill up the boat, even if it is only for a few hours, four days a week.

We tried to get a permit to build a dock, but it looks like that will have to wait until the deal goes through. John has a plan to med-moor *Diamond Lil* to the end of Miss Jessie's wharf next door. That means dropping our anchor out front, to hold us straight while we back into the dock. We will tie off to the shore, not the rickety old dock, but we will be able to use it to get off and on the boat.

I have been lying awake the last few nights imagining myself climbing down the gangplank, like Johnny Depp. After successfully managing to avoid med-mooring in all my seven years and thousands of miles of cruising, suddenly. I find that this is what I'll have to do on Sunday! Yikes, that's only two days away.

Thankfully, Mom and Dad Wood surprised us with a Honda 2000 generator for Christmas last year and delivered it to the island via cruise ship. So, until we get RECO service installed, at least we'll have power. Just a couple of baby steps backward as we move steadily forward.

The plan includes building a house, which John has been scheming and dreaming about for months. Next on the agenda, though, is the stable. We asked Miss Stella, who owns the lot next door, if we could use her property to graze Morena, in exchange for cleaning it and paying her taxes, which are very low here.

"No payment necessary," she said, and she is thrilled to have a horse eat the grass on her yard instead of paying to have it cut. Win, win! I will not have to board Morena at Alana's farm but can keep her right outside the boat.

John has gone down island to shop for supplies. Ned is due with another 10 dory loads of bar mud. The property is so low that when the tide is low we are walking through water.

Garwin is here to spread the bar mud around, thereby raising the property so it is dry and easier to walk on.

Bar mud is black, as mucky as mud can be, and it stinks like the bottom of the sea. It has been dug up from low areas where boats have been going aground. It's just another day in Paradise. Two days until moving day.

September 30, 2012

"You worry too much. It's a piece of cake," John reassured me.

"You always say that, but when we move the boat, after a long time tied to shore, something always goes wrong," I moaned.

"What could go wrong? We are only going a couple of hundred feet. We could just drift there without our engines if we had to. Relax."

As we cast off for our mini-cruise to the rickety little dock we would temporarily med-moor to, I noticed that we weren't moving much. In fact, we weren't moving at all, just drifting. I heard the Captain fiddling with the gear shifters upstairs in the flybridge. Next thing I knew, he was downstairs, driving from our lower navigation station.

"OK, let it down," came the command from inside the boat. I stepped on the windlass foot button. The chain rolled out surprisingly well at first, but before long, the chain coming out of the hold got rustier and rustier. Flakes of rust were flying off as the chain bounced and dropped in fits and spurts. Then it snagged.

"I have a problem up here," I yelled up to John, who was reversing both engines to back us towards the dock.

"What do you mean you have a problem?" he yelled back.

"Hand me the crowbar. The chain is rusty and has jammed," I replied.

Out came the trusty crowbar. I pried and pulled but couldn't loosen the ceased chain. So, the boss came up on the bow and tore into it, finally freeing it. He returned to the controls to back us in while Garwin waited on shore to throw us our lines which John had previously tied to trees, ready for our arrival.

Other than the rusty mess on the bow, the whole process went smoothly, and by 10:30 am, we were in our new home.

The owner of the property, who was here on the island trying to complete the paperwork to close the sale, became ill and ended up in a hospital on the mainland of Honduras with pneumonia. John and I said a few prayers for him (and us).

We can't build the dock or house or connect to the Roatan Electrical Company until we seal the deal, so we're living in the boat and enjoying our little piece of paradise as it is for now. We are thankful that the cooler weather has arrived.

At about 3:00 am, the shrill squeal of the battery alarm jolts us awake, as the batteries die, and we need to get up and switch off the inverter. This means we lose the power to run our fan. If it's not raining, we open the hatch above our bed and hope for a cool breeze. However, it's the rainy season, so it's quite often raining.

We welcome rainy season after the sticky heat of May-September. The boat is dry and cozy. People wear heavy yellow raincoats and dart about in boats between downpours. The mountains bleed rust-colored run-off that turns the clear, turquoise water to murky brown.

On nights when the rain is very heavy, people without boathouses, like us, get up during the night to bail their boats so they don't sink. Invitations come with the phrase "weather permitting" included. It brings back fond memories of our time spent in Guatemala.

Oct 12, 2012

We planned to get our own dog once we moved to the new property. We no longer have the benefit of Joe's dogs to guard the boat and our belongings when we are out.

The universe must have heard us because it seems that we have been adopted by a beautiful, albeit high-strung stray dog. Max showed up, and despite everything we did, he would not leave.

We put him in the skiff and took him over to BJs.

"Oh yes, that's Max. He's been around town for a long time," she told us.

"I think he has people, but they go off sometimes."

Whomever the people were, they didn't seem to be in town because Max just keeps returning to us. He was a beautiful Rhodesian Ridgeback. He insisted on jumping onto the boat, which was already housing two cats, who didn't appreciate his appearance at all.

Finally, we gave in and bought Max a doghouse, some dog food, a collar, and a metal bowl. It looks like we have our dog.

October 21, 2012

Our doghouse now sits empty on the new property. It's a sad sight. It seems that Max did indeed have people, and these people must have returned from wherever they were because Max has left. I was telling my sad tale to the gang at BJs yesterday.

"I know of a family in Lucy Point that has two puppies they want to get rid of," said Mr. Larry.

"The mother dog died. The family has seven children, and the father is sick with diabetes so he can't get much work. They can hardly feed themselves, let alone the puppies, so they really need a home."

When the band packed up at 4:00 pm, a bunch of us climbed into our respective dinghies and skiffs, headed under the little footbridge, and followed the waterway to Lucy Point. We all climbed out on the dock at Orlando's bar. Larry went off to look for the family with the puppies while the rest of us ordered a drink.

He returned shortly with a couple of children and two puppies. They looked nothing like each other. One was brown and fluffy, with a collie type pointed snout. The other one was black and white, with short hair. He ran directly towards John.

It was love at first sight. Both John and I fell for the black and white puppy. We paid the children 200 lempiras ($10.00), and they ran off with huge smiles on their faces.

Theodore has joined our family. We now have 2 cats and one puppy living on the boat. He will be an outside dog eventually, but the large, vicious dogs next door at

Lourdes's place make us nervous so we will keep him in the boat for now.

I slept with the little guy in my arms last night. I think he is not yet six weeks old but with no mother dog, he is better off with us. The first time we fed him, it brought tears to my eyes. I don't think he has had much to eat for the first few weeks of his life.

Nov 6, 2012

Morena will be eight months old on Nov 12th. It was time to wean her and bring her home. Richard McNab, who lives in Oak Ridge and has two horses himself, offered to bring her from the farm to Oak Ridge in his horse trailer.

She didn't want to go into the trailer, but with several strong men helping, it wasn't a problem. They simply picked her up and put her in.

It isn't far to travel, but for a young filly who has never been away from her mother or the farm, the walk down through Spanish Hill and Oak Ridge would be terrifying.

The end of the road came at the little footbridge that leads to the point. We unloaded her from the trailer, and between several of us, we managed to walk her home to the Point. She balked at the entrance to the bridge, but Julio, who is as strong as an ox, just lifted her rear end in the air and pushed her along.

We walked her along the narrow walkway that follows the shore, past Miss Sandy's, to our place. Her new stall was ready, thanks to John and Garwin, who dragged the lumber and zinc from town in the skiff and built it last week.

Dec 31, 2012

I have been invited to speak at the Toronto Boat show about our first two adventures on *Diamond Lil*, the loop trip and our two winters in the Bahamas. Now that the show is only a couple of weeks away, it's sinking in that I am really going to do this. I will give two presentations – one on each of my two books and have a chance to sell the books at the show.

Jan 4, 2013

We love our new location, but the one thing I was really missing was my office. By that, I mean the great room in the house at Joe's place. Living with your spouse 24/7 in a small area, like a boat, is something you adapt to, and we get along very well in our little cave. However, trying to write or work when you are sitting two feet apart and sharing table space isn't quite so much fun.

We explored the options and decided to rent a cute little house, three doors down from us on the Point, from my friend Alana. The rent, like most costs down here, is minimal. The whole house is only $100/month.

Down in the little house, it is breezy, about 20 degrees cooler than the boat, bright, and quiet. There is no generator running in the background to muddy up my narrations that I am working on. Over and over and over, I read the same lines from the book, with nobody to irritate me except the birds chirping outside my windows. John doesn't have to listen to me recite the story over and over, for six to eight hours a day. He surely knows it by heart.

In the rare event that the power goes out, like the second day I worked in my office, I must make the 60-second walk back to the boat, along the sea, under massive swamp dogwood trees, past my tropical gardens, past my horse, who is grazing peacefully in front of the sea, past Theodore, who is so excited to have me home that he jumps up on me, and work in the boat.

Feb 15, 2013

"We are invited to Alex and Marilyn's wedding on Saturday," said John, as I walked out of my bedroom, sleepy-eyed. He is normally up before me and had been reading the posts on Facebook.

"Which Saturday?" I asked.

"I'm not sure. It doesn't say," he said. "It's at Chuck and Barb's house."

Alex's first wife, Kelly, had succumbed to cancer. We were all saddened to lose her. She was a lively part of our little group.

After spending some time grieving, Alex had met a new woman on eHarmony. She had come to the island, fallen in love with Alex, and fortunately, our island. She was here to stay, and they were getting married – tomorrow as it turned out!

You just never know what the new day will bring here in Roatan.

Feb 20, 2013

I was looking for a restaurant to feature in the next issue of the real estate newsletter that I write for Alex. I was also itching to check out the new Gio's Restaurant in Flower's Bay.

Our first stop, as we headed down-island, was in Coxen

Hole, to meet up with a "friend," who had renewed John's slightly overdue passport for him at a fraction of the cost of the sharks at the airport. He had accidentally gone over his 90 days, and the fine for that is steep.

With business wrapped up, we stopped for lunch at Gio's on the Beach - Gio's new restaurant in Flower's Bay, which opened about a year ago. The original Gio's Restaurant, in French Harbour, was opened by Giovanni Silvestri Ferez and his wife, Rosa, almost 20 years ago. John and I enjoyed meals there several times a few years ago when we anchored the boat down at French Cay.

I was looking for a restaurant to feature in the next issue of the newsletter that I write for Alex. I was also itching to check out the new Gio's. I wanted to try the signature dish, King Crab. It had been voted one of the 30 Wonders of Honduras and the first wonder in the culinary category.

We noticed that a few of the items on the menu were named after well-known islanders. The "Eldon's Special" is a dish that was created for frequent customer Eldon Hyde, who favored a combination of crab, lobster, and shrimp. "Charly Big Fish" was a dish inspired by good friend Charly Frissel, who preferred a large, hot dish of grilled shellfish and vegetables.

After an appetizer of conch chowder, we shared the Eldon's Special. The presentation was amazing, the service excellent, and the setting ideal. I had been told that the food in the French Harbour location was better, and I'd be tempted to agree. The lobster and crab were both overcooked.

Next stop: West End. The funky little island town always strikes me as a place that could only exist in a novel, but there it is! Lounging on the beach, with a cold Salva Vida in hand, I was relieved to see boats anchored in the bay once again. Last we heard, the mooring balls had all been removed, and boats were no longer permitted to stay there.

On the way home, we stopped in Sandy Bay at the Blue Parrot, where despite our seafood feast a few hours earlier, we could not resist what we believe is THE BEST jerk chicken and rice and beans on the island. It's always fun to stop and visit Carol and Annie and observe the odd mix of Sandy Bay gringos that frequent the place.

No matter where we go on this island - north, south, east, or west - the view is simply the BEST!

March 18, 2013

What better way to celebrate my birthday could there possibly be than a boat cruise with friends? We gladly accepted the invitation to join Larry and Karen Coon and a group of our friends aboard their dive boat *Islander* for a cruise to the Pigeon Cays.

Armed with snorkeling gear and bathing suits, we met at BJs Backyard, just across the channel from where we live. It was an 8:00 am departure, a little early for the captain and me. We are up at the crack of dawn each day, but trying to actually be somewhere that early, well that's stressful.

After a brief stop to pick up Wendy, Hugh, and their kayaks in Calabash Bight, we headed east, past the end of the island, to the Pigeon Cays, three tiny islets that seem to be in the middle of nowhere. The water was crystal clear, as we anchored within swimming distance of one pristine, little island.

After a great water workout, we headed back west, stopping at the scenic little island of St. Helene, considered part of Roatan, although it is separated by a narrow mangrove channel. Lunch was served on the beach, by local residents, Kevit and his wife. He caught the dorado and grouper, and she cooked it, along with rice and beans, potato salad, and vegetables. For dessert, we had fresh fruit.

After lunch, a stroll along the picturesque island was in order. The photo opportunities were endless, as we wandered along the sandy trail that led along the shore.

On the return trip, we caught a glimpse of the *Corwith Cramer*, a research vessel manned by college students, earning credits as they travel the high seas. Captain Cootie raced across the sea towards her so that we could get close enough for pictures.

I was exhausted by the time we pulled into BJs and wandered inside to have a cold one there before heading home. It's tradition. It was after 5:00 pm by the time we crawled into the boat - sticky, salty, burned, exhausted, but what a great day we had!

May 25, 2013
4:00 am

"May I see your return ticket, please, Ma'am?" asked the agent at the Delta Airline check-in desk.

"This is my return ticket," I answered.

"No, I mean your return ticket to Canada. I am afraid we cannot let you board without it."

"I don't have one," I insisted. "How could I? I have no idea when I am returning to Canada."

"You need to produce either a return ticket or a Honduran residency card. Honduras can legally deny you entry if you have no return ticket," she said. "If that happens, the airline is liable for a huge fine."

"We have an up-to-date cruising permit for our boat," I told her. "We live down there most of the year on our boat. We are in the country legally. They won't deny me entry. Please! We have been flying there for years. I know they will let me in."

For years, I had carried our cruising permit, stamped and dated by the Honduran immigration officials, in my laptop bag. Nobody had ever asked to see it. Not in eight years of flying back and forth, often several times each year. For some unexplainable reason, I had not brought it with me this time. I explained this to the woman behind the desk.

"If you can have the permit faxed to me," I can let your board," she told me.

"It's 4:00 am here," I moaned. That means that it is 2:00 am in Roatan. My husband, who has the certificate, is sound asleep. Even if he did hear the phone, we don't own a fax machine. The only fax machine in our town is at the Shrimp Factory, which will not open until morning."

"Please step aside, Ma'am, until you can provide the cruising permit or a return ticket. You are holding up the line."

"What line?" I demanded, becoming increasingly irritated and raising my voice. "There is nobody behind me."

"Ma'am, if you are going to be difficult, I will have to call security," she warned me.
Tears began to stream down my face.

"You don't understand," I said, again in a louder voice than she found acceptable.

"I have a wedding to go to tomorrow. I need to get on that plane." Rb and Bryan were getting married, and we had been invited to the wedding.

"Step out of the line, Ma'am," repeated the woman.

I looked over, helplessly at the two security officers who were standing by and had heard the entire exchange. One of them smiled in my direction, obviously feeling for my dilemma.

"Ma'am, the gate closes at 5:00 am, one hour before your 6:00 am flight. I suggest you either have that certificate faxed very soon or purchase a return ticket to Canada."

By this time, I was crying and gasping, having only had a few hours of sleep at Lisa's house before she dropped me off at 4:00 am. I plopped down on a seat and texted her, hoping that she had left her phone on before going back to bed. Then, I called John. Despite it being the middle of the night, he did hear the phone and listened while I relayed what was happening. Then I called Lisa again.

"Lisa, what am I going to do?" I wailed. "I will just die if I miss Rb's wedding! I don't have enough money on my visa to buy a return ticket."

"That's okay," Lisa said. I will go online quickly and buy you a ticket. You can pay me back."

I thanked her profusely and waited, none too patiently, for her to text back with the good news that I had a return ticket and would get on the plane. I watched the clock, edging closer and closer to the 5:00 am cut-off time.

Finally, Lisa texted me back with the ticket number and I rushed to the agent's desk with it.

"I am sorry, Ma'am, but I need the confirmation number as well."

I texted Lisa once again and asked if she could get the confirmation number. There was a delay and by the time she got it, the clock had rolled past 5:00 am.

"I am sorry, said the agent, "but boarding is now closed. You will have to take the next flight to Roatan."
"When is that," I asked.

"Let's see," she said, as she searched her computer.

"The next flight combination to Roatan is a week from today, Saturday, June 2nd at 6:00 am. There are flights to Atlanta, but nothing from there to Roatan until then."

"But the wedding is tomorrow?" I pleaded. "Can't you just please get me a flight to Atlanta? I will pay for the flight to Roatan from there."

"I am sorry, Ma'am. We can only replace the exact flight combination that you purchased. We cannot fly you part of the way there."

I had no choice but to call Lisa, who returned to the airport to pick me up. I was stuck in Canada for another week. We spent the morning canceling the return ticket.

July 18, 2013

If attendance at Cal's Temporary Cantina's one-year anniversary party is any indication, there are many islanders that are relieved that one of our favorite east end eateries is anything but temporary.

Cal's Facebook page has dropped the temporary from the restaurant's name, a huge relief for those of us who plan our "down-island" shopping trips around Cal's opening hours. He's only open Tuesday through Friday, which, for me, makes a Monday shopping trip out of the question. We love to stop on the way home to see what delectable dishes Carl has scribbled on his colorful menu board.

The FB invitation boasted a live band, cash bar, and free *Bocas* (appetizers).

"We should arrive early," warned John. I had to agree, for I expected a huge turnout. Indeed, the roadway was already lined with cars when we arrived as crowds from all over the island poured in.

However, Carl had somehow managed to complete the construction on his expansion, literally overnight. We had been for lunch just the day before, and here, just one day later, the seating capacity had been increased by about 400 - 500% with the addition of a second seating area just outside the original building. Despite the large turnout, there was plenty of seating room for everyone.

When Carl began to serve the *Bocas*, we were not
disappointed. These were no ordinary *hors d'eouvres*.
Large platters of home-made corn chips with decadent
dips were followed by hot, fresh tortillas with chicken,
all the fixings, and a delicious seafood salad.

Three large serving dishes appeared next, with
vegetable lasagna, a rice dish, and steaming meatballs
in a mouth-watering sauce. Finally, a large cake was
served. As always, it tasted as wonderful as it looked.

Bobby Rieman, one of my favorite island entertainers,
set the mood with his lively mix of reggae and island
tunes. I requested a song that he wrote himself, called
"Sin Saldo." The lyrics poke fun at the way islanders
have grown dependent on their pay-as-you-go cell
phones.

Aug 12, 2013

The months whiz by. I am thankful for many things in
my life. Having so much free time is near the top of the
list. Still, as much free time as I have, there is so much
to do that I still don't feel like I ever have enough.

Our morning begins around 5:30 or 6:00. Sleeping on
the water, with an open hatch above our heads, means
that we feel and hear morning arrive before we open our
eyes. Boat traffic increases. The water becomes
choppier. Dogs bark more.

We hear Darcy, across the canal, pulling up to the dock
outside his little *tienda* in his skiff. We hear his many
guard dogs barking. They have been loose in his fenced
compound during the night, guarding his store, and he
has arrived to put them in their kennels for the day. He

doesn't open right away, but he turns on his music. It wafts across the water to our boat.

John is usually out of bed first. He unlocks our back door and slides it open. It's noisy, and Morena whinnies as soon as she hears it. It's comforting to me, lying half-awake in bed, to hear her because I know she is safe and sound.

John steps down onto the aft deck and fills the kettle for our coffee from the five-gallon jug of drinking water that we keep out there. There is no room in the boat for something that large.

While the kettle boils and I pretend that I'm still asleep, John walks out to see the animals. I feel guilty but too cozy to be the first out, usually. I drift back off to sleep, despite the clackety dories passing by not far from my head and the barking dogs, for these are the sounds of my life.

I feel the motion of John stepping back on to the boat and hear and smell him make the coffee. Honduran coffee trumps sleep at this point, and I wander out. I step out of the boat, walk down the dock to the shore, give Morena her breakfast of *Omalina* horse chow and say good morning. Then it's back to the boat for coffee and the internet. After a while, I put on the kettle for our second cup of coffee. While it boils, I make the bed, shower, and get dressed. We enjoy our second cup of steamy Honduran coffee, check our messages, and enjoy the coolest part of the day.

After coffee #2, it's outside for me. I put on Morena's halter, tie her to the fence outside her stall, and groom her. Four times a week, on Monday, Wednesday, Friday, and Saturday, we get town water until 11 am. That is the time to water our many plants – the only time.

Two long hoses are joined together to reach all around our property, to the boat, to the empty lot next door, and to Miss Jessie's place. I water my plants, which are spread out over our property and the empty lot next door, and then I water Miss Jessie's. It takes about an hour, and I love it. It's so hot by this time that I wear a hat and long-sleeved shirt, or at least I try to. Some of the plants are in full sun and need a lot of water, so I position the hose at the base of the plant and duck into the shade while it gets watered. I spray all the leaves on every plant, to rid them of the salt spray that covers everything. Morena follows me around while I water the plants.

When I open Miss Jessie's gate, Morena follows me into her yard. She rolls in her favorite spot, then grazes while I water her plants. When I'm done watering and go home, I leave her there for the day. Miss Jessie is thrilled to never have to hire a man to "chop" her lot. Most people don't use lawnmowers here. They just hire a man with a machete to chop their grass and weeds. But, Morena does this, and Miss Jessie loves her company.

By now it's about 9:00 am. By this time, I need my second shower of the day. My shirt is soaking wet and plastered to my skin, so I shower and change, perhaps have some breakfast, or at least a cold iced tea.

Now, I must decide what to do. It's easy to stay outside ‑ raking, weeding, pruning, and planting. It's also easy to sit beside my fan and play computer games. It's not so easy to walk down to my office and work on my latest book, but my conscience makes me do it.

I should clean the boat. It's a mess. There are power tools everywhere, left from John's constant projects. I whine and ask him to put them away, but no, there is another project, so why put them away. AHHHHH. So, I ignore the piles of man‑stuff and retreat to either my uncluttered, peaceful office or outside, to my plants.

Time passes by. John is a man of few words. Usually, the next thing he says to me is "What do you want to do for lunch?"

In jest, I reply, "Chinese take‑out" or "Let's order in," because, of course, we can't do either here. The closest thing to take‑out is either a fried chicken dinner or a *baleada* from across the harbor, but I'm trying to lose weight before I ride Morena next March, so that just won't do.

Between our thriving social life, my horse, and my growing garden, I rarely find the time anymore to work on book #3. But, it's time to get back to pursuing this goal.

Do we own this property yet, you ask? Well, no, but we are eternally hopeful. It should be any day now. It's been over a year since our offer was accepted and almost a year since we moved here.

We can't get permits from the municipality to build our dock, our wall around the property, or our house yet, so we plug away at the jobs we can do and wait patiently.

Sept 23, 2013

"I know we agreed that we were not in the market for a second dog," said John over the phone. He was on a down-island shopping trip. I had stayed at home to work on my book when he called me.

"Right," I said, guessing that this was leading somewhere.

"I am here at Rick's," he continued. Rick's was what we normally referred to Carniagro, the agriculture and pet supply store in French Harbour. He had stopped in to buy a bag of horse feed.

"There are two Rottweiler puppies for sale here. They are way overpriced, and I know the timing isn't great. I feel so badly for them. They are in a large birdcage, outside, in full sun. They don't even have any water. There is a male and a female. I'm sure Theodore would love the female. Maybe Miss Sandy is right, and he won't wander so much if he has another dog to keep him company," he reasoned.

"You say they are way overpriced. How much are they asking?"

"He is asking $150.00 US. I can try to talk him down. They are really nice-looking dogs," he said.

"Ok," I told him. "Get her if you want to. What the heck?"

Theodore had taken to wandering into town. We were constantly receiving phone calls from Carmen, BJs husband, that he was there. John would run over in the boat and bring him home. He had even killed a chicken on one of his forays into town. We were worried that an angry neighbor would shoot or poison him.

'Y'all need to get him a friend," Miss Sandy had told us, on several occasions. "Another dog, preferably a female.

"I don't think so," Miss Sandy, I had argued, over and over.

"We already have a horse, one dog, and six cats. We can't build a house until we get the paperwork for the property."

A short while later, John returned from town. I watched as he crossed the channel and pulled up to the dock. On the back seat, beside him, was my new printer. On his lap, was the puppy.

"They say she is a Rotty," John told me, "but I don't think she is purebred. She looks more like a Doberman to me. Look how pointed her nose is."

Theodore wore a grin from ear to ear when he ran out to meet John and saw the puppy. I am sure he thinks we got her for him. I guess he is right.

Nov 29, 2013

It's a good thing we didn't go far today. Several times a
week, we suffer from cabin fever and need to get out. A
trip across the narrow waterway to BJ's is always a
pleasure. Many of the boat-access only residents take
advantage of her parking arrangements. She charges a
small monthly fee to park their vehicle in her large lot.
She has plenty of dock space for boats to tie to while the
owners are out and about. Her place is open 365 days a
year, so someone, usually BJ herself, is there to ensure
the safety of their boats and vehicles.

Friday is a busy day, often with standing room only,
which is fine, because we have many friends to wander
about and mingle with. BJ is always standing in her
corner, behind the bar, marking the drink and meal
purchases in her book. The place gets packed so she is
busy making bills and taking payment. She has little
time to chat.

However, on any other day of the week, BJ is more than
happy to sit and chat. She has a million stories if you
take the time to stop and sit and listen. Some of my
favorite tales are the ones from her youth, when she and
her good friend, Janet Lafferty, nicknamed JD, lived in
Key West. Those were the years when Jimmy Buffet
still played in bars for free drinks, she told us.

BJ is a small woman, slight of build but not of
character. She wears her medium brown hair cut short.
Her brown eyes sparkle behind her eyeglasses as her
face breaks into a huge smile whenever we walk
through her door.

Don't ever cross her though, we had heard. What she lacks in size, she makes up for in attitude. I will never forget the very first conversation we had with BJ, back when we first moved to Oak Ridge.

We had ventured over to her bar, tied our little rubber dinghy to the dock, and stepped in through the always-open door. We parked ourselves on two of the bar stools and ordered a drink.

"Where are you from?" she asked us, as we began to chat.

"Originally, we are from Canada. We live on the powerboat over on the Point," I said, pointing across the channel at *Diamond Lil*."

"Well," BJ said, not missing a beat. "You are the only ones from that Point welcome in here."

She certainly doesn't beat around the bush, I thought to myself at the time.

We were sitting on the little bench on a particularly quiet day, chatting with BJ, when *Diamond Lil* started drifting sideways. The wind had pulled out a piling, broke our main anchor chain, and another anchor line.

We rushed back across the channel and called our friend, Tyller Hynds, who brought his boat over to help us. Ed and Julie graciously came to our rescue by lending us an anchor. When the weather clears, we will pay a diver to find three of our anchors, which have all gone missing over the last few days.

Boat traffic passes by very close, so perhaps a line was unintentionally cut. Or, not totally impossible, someone has stolen our anchors.

Garwin, helping us to move our plants to the new property

Diamond Lil, in her new home, just a few feet from her old home

Garwin, spreading bar mud on the new property

Filling in the low land and the picnic table John and Garwin built

John, bringing home the new puppy

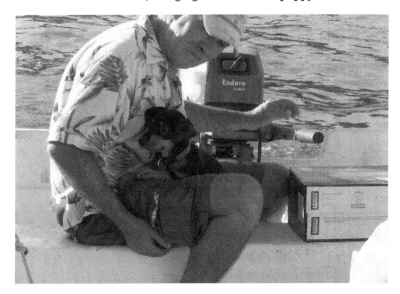

People came to see if it was true that there was a horse on the Point

Chapter 14

January 16, 2014

Finally, after 18 months of work, I have published my third book. Diamond Lil Does the Rio Dulce has been born. My first two books each took a year to write. This third one took a year and a half. Our group of friends continues to grow, and we spend more time attending parties and events than we did in years past.

January 30, 2014

Literally speaking, I am back in the saddle again, although for very short periods at a time. I have been on Morena's back eight times now, seven times bareback, and most recently, with the saddle on. It's a little frightening to think of hitting the ground at my age, so I'm taking it slow and being very cautious.

So far, she hasn't minded at all, except once, when our newest dog, Brown Dog, decided that she looked, or smelled, like a female dog and tried to mount her. That made for a quick dismount. Brown Dog just showed up, much like Max did, but unlike Max, this dog stayed.

We were not at all in the market for a third dog. BJ recognized this dog and wasn't quite sure where he had come from. He was just a street dog who everyone called Brown Dog. A street dog that just would not leave. He followed us everywhere. When we got in the skiff to go out, he swam behind us. It was a constant matter of returning him home.

It's been a very wet rainy season here in Roatan. The weather has been cooler, which is a pleasant change from the steamy summer. It is beginning to dry up, and we are enjoying the nicest weather of the year. F February 16, 2014 No matter how many times I travel from Roatan to Ontario and back, it's always a mind-boggling experience. Within a few short hours, I am transported from nose-stinging, ear-biting cold and heavy, grey skies to a tropical paradise. From below freezing temperatures in Toronto, as I slid my toonie into the slot in the luggage cart dispenser at the airport, to 61 degrees F when we landed in Miami, to 78 degrees F when we touched down in Roatan.

The captain was there waiting for me, as always. We squeezed my luggage into the back seat of our pickup truck, alongside the cooler full of ice, bags of dog and cat food, and two cartons full of my new books.

Great timing! The books arrived at BJ's Backyard late on Friday, and I was here by 1:00 pm on Saturday.

Feb 22, 2014

I am thrilled to report that we matched Brown Dog with Mr. Dwayne of Jonesville, from Alberta, Canada. We will miss this sweet, devoted dog, but peace has been restored to our little piece of paradise. We hope he is happy in his new, eight-acre home

March 6, 2014

Spending two weeks in Canada in February made me appreciate our winter paradise that much more.

"How can you stand to go to Canada in the winter?" many of my friends from Roatan ask. I am always happy to see my family and two weeks of ice, cold, and snow is good medicine.

I am very thankful to have escaped the Great White North for the past eight winters. March is the perfect time of year here on the island. The rainy season is over. The hot weather hasn't quite arrived - well except for the odd day here and there. Mostly, it's perfect - sunny and warm with refreshing trade winds blowing from the east.

Our boating pals from Lake Simcoe, Deb and John, are coming to visit from March 10th-20th. We are thrilled. My John introduced me to the boating life and his group of boating pals back in 2001, the summer before we were married. I thought I had died and gone to heaven, as we rafted up with all these fun people. We had our very own Redneck Yacht Club - sharing meals, boat drinks, fishing, and listening to music, on our home lake.

John and Deb visited us for ten days on Diamond Lil in 2005. "My hero," John said, as he shook my John's hand when we met them at the Ft. Myers airport. Mom and Dad had lent us their van to drive them from the airport to the Burnt Store Marina, where Diamond Lil was docked. Deb and John's eyes popped out of their heads as we led them down the main dock and towards our finger dock at the ritzy marina. John dropped his luggage on our back deck and just kept walking, drooling as he took in all the sailing vessels in the harbor.

"We waited until you arrived to decide on our itinerary. We can either keep the boat here at the marina and make day trips to the beautiful islands in this area. They are famous for their plentiful shells," I said, over dinner at the Porto Bello Restaurant.

"However, the weather is cooler here than I hoped for. The other option is to make the trip down to the Keys and anchor in Boot Key Harbor. It's beautiful and much warmer than it is here. You would need to rent a car to get back to the airport in Fort Myers, because we don't want to bring the boat all the way back up north. From there, we are Bahamas bound."

Looking at each other, over the table, in unison, they said, "Let's go to the Keys!"

The 100-foot wide channel between Keewaydin Island and Little Marco Island was where we anchored for the night after our first day of cruising southward. The next day, we cruised to Marathon and spent the rest of their holidays in the Keys, including New Year's Eve in Key West. What a great night we had!

A few of our original Lake Simcoe boating crowd dreamed the dream of leaving the winters behind and traveling south on our boats. Our dream came true. John and Deb's dream also came true. We had spoiled them for any kind of normal life. Just like us, they sold their home in Keswick, Ontario and began the search for the perfect boat. Sweet Surrender was their ticket out of frosty Ontario.

We are very excited to have Deb and John come to visit us here in Roatan. They are considering investing in property on the island, so we will enjoy showing them around. It's the social season here, and we already have two boat trips and one amazing party lined up to take them to.

This past Saturday, after a shopping trip down-island, we drove to the east end of the island, to La Sirena, a restaurant/bar in Camp Bay, for the afternoon. We ran into our friend, Martina, who invited us to dinner at her east-end resort, Lost Moose Guesthouse.

John had met Martina at Bryan and RBs wedding; the wedding that I missed when the United Airlines clerk denied me access to my flight back to Roatan, so I had not.

Martina was born in Germany and had immigrated to Canada with her family when she was a child. She grew up in Gravenhurst, Ontario. Like us, she had owned a cottage on Three Mile Lake, in Muskoka. She had driven with her son and two large dogs, all the way from Ontario to Honduras, then come by ship from the mainland to Roatan.

Now, she lives in Port Royal. After a scenic drive to the east end of the island, we climbed the long, steep hill that led to Port Royal. As we climbed higher and higher,

I felt more like I was back in Ontario, surrounded by pine and oak trees, than on a tropical island. Her house sat perched atop a steep hill. In the valley below, I spotted scores of mature lime and mango trees, with a backdrop of the dense jungle, and beyond that, the shining sea of Port Royal.

It was an open concept floor plan, with the kitchen and living area in the center and two guest rooms off to each side. In addition, there were two more bedrooms and a large living area on the second floor.

On the back wall of the kitchen stood an enormous, commercial stainless steel DCS stove. It was a beast – 60" wide, with six burners, two ovens, a salamander, and flat-top. An L-shaped wooden bar, varnished to a shine, surrounded the cooking area, so she could visit with her guests while she made dinner.

We perched on bar stools to chat while she worked her wonders. She was a chef by trade, so we were in for a treat. Along the front of the living area was a stone wall made from island rock that doubled as a planter. Contrasting shades of bougainvillea cascaded over the wall in a dazzling display of color.

Martina was an attractive woman, of medium height, with dark brown hair and brown eyes. I was envious of her olive complexion, deeply tanned, compared to my red-headed, white, freckled skin.

After a delightful night out, we arrived home late. When I opened the fridge to put away our groceries, I knew trouble had come knocking. A sense of deja vu overcame me, as I walked down to my office to put the groceries in the fridge down there. The next day, Captain Fix-It went to work, but alas, the fridge was no more. It was a Norcold fridge which we had shipped to Bimini from Miami back in 2006. Boaters nickname them Nevercold because they never are.

Rather than pay $1,400.00 US plus shipping costs to import another Nevercold fridge to the island, we decided to shop here for a regular house fridge. However, we had to find one that would fit into the raised opening above our diesel tank and below the electronics for the lower helm station – not an easy undertaking. John went down the island, on a mission, with his measurements and tape measure in hand.

He returned with the verdict. There was only one non-white fridge on the island that would fit into the small space available and three different stores carried it, all at different prices.

Our stove and microwave are black and stainless, so white was out of the question. The fridge available was pewter - or grey. I went along on the next trip and haggled with the salesclerk, who gave me another 1,000 lempiras ($50.00) off the price.

Shopping on the island is sort of like swimming upstream. We asked the salesclerk if she had another fridge, in a box. We didn't want the floor model since we had to transport it along bumpy roads in the back of our pickup truck, then put it into our skiff from a dock, take it back out, and get it from our dock into Diamond Lil.

"We have no system," the clerk whined. Why would they? The store has only been open for a couple of months.

"Come here," she yelled, from behind a computer desk. I thought she was calling the male clerk to go get the fridge.

"I think she means you," said John. Yes, sure enough, she had called to me - the customer - in that irritated fashion.

I sat down across from her while she fumbled around on the computer, huffing, and puffing.

"Wait here," she barked, as she went off in search of help.

Like Hell, I thought, as I got up from the chair she had attempted to confine me to and browsed around the store for a while. Finally, she returned and managed to input the information into her computer. She printed me an invoice and said, "Go over there." Not "Please go over there to the caja ma'am," as one might expect.

In Canada or the US, you just pay cash at the check-out. Here, once you receive the printed invoice, you must take it to a *caja* , or cashier. Apparently, they don't trust the staff with cash.

The girl at the *caja* fumbled around for a while, and finally, printed a second invoice. She removed it and stared at it for the longest time as if it was her graduation certificate or something. Perhaps it's the first day of invoice printing for her. After she stared at it for a while, she found something she didn't like and proceeded to print another one. Finally, I paid her the cash - in US dollars. That totally confused the cashier, and it took a while longer to get our change.

You would think that during all this, they would have sent for the fridge to be brought from inventory. Not here. At this point, they called for someone to get the fridge. John sensed my annoyance and said he'd wait for the fridge while I walked up the street to buy a big pot for my newest plant. Good call. By the time I returned, the fridge was in the back of the truck, ready to go.

After a stop for lunch at Cal's, one of our favorite eateries on the island, we drove to Oak Ridge. John backed the truck up next to the dock at the parking lot where we leave it parked.

"Do you need help? I'll send Ren over to help you," Martina yelled out from next door at BJs, having watched us pull in with our heavy load.

"It's not heavy. We can do it," said John.

"No way," I said. Ren is BIG. Him vs me - to help John haul it out of the pickup truck, onto the dock, into the skiff, out of the skiff - an easy choice.

He also offered to help us pull the old fridge out of Diamond Lil and put the new one in. I was relieved and invited him and his wife, Shannon, over for some cold beer.

While John chatted with them outside, I quickly emptied the old fridge of the foul, rotting mess of food that I still hadn't thrown out. YES, I know I should have done it before this point. I piled the foulest garbage in one sink, choking and gagging as I worked. John popped his head in to see how I was doing. I begged him to keep everyone away while I finished. I felt Cal's delicious Dorado lunch creep up my throat, and before I knew it, I was throwing up on top of the pile of rotten food in the sink.

After cleaning the sink, taking a quick shower, and changing my clothes, I joined our company outside, wearing a smiling face and bearing more cold beer. John had already removed the hardware from the back door to make the opening wider. I remembered having to do that for the last fridge, and this one was precisely the same width. I did not dare watch while John and Ren wrestled the old fridge out and the new fridge in. I was so thankful that Ren had helped us with the job.

This fridge is a MABE model, so I nicknamed it MAYBE. Maybe it will keep the food cold. Maybe I can keep my beer in there, instead of a cooler full of ice. Maybe I can even make ice!

So far, we are thrilled with the MABE fridge. It has a super vacuum seal. After you close it once, don't dare try to open it again. We could travel the roughest seas, and this fridge is guaranteed not to fall open. John had to secure it to the back wall so I didn't pull it right out trying to open it. MABE you can open it, MABE not!

Mar 8, 2014

I had a dream a few nights ago that Brown Dog came back. I guess some dreams do come true. John patiently loaded him into the skiff and drove him back to Jonesville.

Mar 20, 2014

He's back! Brown Dog came back for a second time. Once again, John drove him to Jonesville in the boat. Half an hour later, he was back, this being the third time. Overland and swimming at times, I imagine this crazy dog, making the trek from Jonesville to Oak Ridge in half an hour.

Mar 25, 2014

We have given up on returning Brown Dog to Jonesville. I guess he is here to stay. He will not stop fighting with the neighbor's dogs. When he does, Theodore and Sophie join in. This must stop if he is to stay.

When the fight is over, even when he is bitten and bleeding, clearly the loser in the match, he paws at the ground, like a bull about to charge. He reminds me of Sylvester Stallone in the movie "Rocky." Hence, his new name, Rocky. Tomorrow, Rocky will say goodbye to his *cajones*.

The World vets are on the island, volunteering their time, and he has an appointment with a scalpel. M Mar 27, 2014 Brown Dog, aka Rocky, is slowly healing from his surgery. "Keep him out of the water for ten days," instructed the vet. Oh no, I thought to myself. Just one of Rocky's quirks of character was his habit of only relieving himself in the sea. Never on land. Ten days was going to be rough. I led him around our property for ages.

He tugged towards the shore by Miss Jessie's house, his usual in-water toilet. I dragged him away. Finally, he would squat and do his business. I had to confine him to the back deck of Diamond Lil to keep him from wandering into the sea.

When he jumped over the transom to get out, I had to resort to tying him up inside the back deck of the boat.

"He goes crazy when you leave to go to your office, John told me," when I returned from my days' work.

The next day, when I strolled down the short walk to my office, two doors away, I took Rocky with me and shut him up inside with me while I worked. He was happy while he was with me. The whistle I heard as the clock neared 12 noon meant that John had lunch almost ready. I saved my work and locked the door.

"I won't be long, Rocky," I told him, as I walked under the front balcony.

I left the front door open since it was unlikely that anyone would scale the wall to the balcony. We had just sat down to lunch when I heard the most horrific yelp from the direction of my office. I knew what had happened. I scrambled out of the boat and ran towards my office. Before I got a few feet from the boat, there was Rocky, limping on his bloody, mangled foot.

He had lunged from the second story balcony rather than have me leave him behind. I felt sick with guilt and regret. Why hadn't I brought poor Rocky home with me for lunch?

Luckily, our friend, Heather Koziol, who is an operating room nurse by trade, offered to come to our boat to treat Rocky. Heather travels back and forth between Roatan and different cities all over the US, where she works, usually at a different hospital in a different city each time.

Her husband, Ron, stays here most of the time, building what will become the first of two casitas they have planned. After that, they will build their house and rent the casitas to tourists. Heather bounded on to the boat, wearing her usual huge smile and bright red hair. She was always smiling, often chuckling with enthusiasm. She removed my attempt at a bandage and cleaned, bandaged and splinted Rocky's leg. He will remain tied to the ladder in the back deck of our boat, a prisoner here, until his leg, in addition to his neutering incision, is healed.

June 2, 2014

Washing our clothes has become a challenge since we left Joe's dock and moved to our new spot, two lots away. We left not only his dock but his washing machine.

"I'll do your laundry," offered Karen Coon, a friend from Oak Ridge.

Karen loved to walk and one of her favorite walks was over the little footbridge at Silent Springs and along the seashore on the south coast of the Point, to our property. Karen always came bearing gifts for Morena.

She and her husband, Larry, drank a lot of fruit smoothies. She saved all the peels and all her vegetable refuse for Morena. She froze it, and when it came time to visit, she lugged down bags of frozen fruit treats. Morena was like a kid in a candy store when Karen came to visit.

Karen and Larry had moved here from Oregon. She wore her thick auburn hair cut shoulder length with a fringe of bangs. She was famous for her mouth-watering carrot cakes. She would tirelessly make them for one friend after another and cart them down the little avenue from her place to BJs on a Friday afternoon.

We all sang happy birthday to whoever was celebrating that week. Sometimes there was more than one birthday person. Karen cut the cake and shared it with everyone in the crowd. Larry had taught himself to play the bass guitar a couple of years ago and had hence joined the Banditos. He was famous for his love of tie-dye clothing. I like to call him Tie-Dye Guy.

Larry looked every bit the rock and roll star with his long mane of thick, grey hair, with a thick, long grey beard and thick, grey mustache to match. His wardrobe did not include shoes. He was a barefoot kind of guy.

At first, I was stunned by Karen's offer to do our laundry. How could I possibly hand over our stinky, dirty clothes and expect her to wash and dry them?

"No, really. I love doing laundry. Just until you figure something out."

Thank you, Saint Karen. I felt embarrassed every time we dropped off our green garbage bag full of dirty laundry, and I mean dirty. We were working like dogs on the new property and in this tropical, humid, heat. Well, you can imagine.

"We can't go on asking Karen to do our laundry forever, honey," I pleaded to John one day.

"There is water in my office. It looks like that little room outside on the back balcony is for a washing machine. We could hang lines on the front balcony. The wind would dry the clothes in no time," I added.

Thus, began our washing machine saga on the island of Roatan. Our first purchase was a used washing machine from the Molineros store in downtown Coxen Hole. The man assured us that it was in working condition. If it failed to work, he would refund our money. Of this I was doubtful. There are few money-back guarantees here.

We loaded it into the truck, hauled it home to BJs, loaded it into the skiff, and carried it across the waterway to the little wharf outside my office. We hauled it up the steps, and John went to work installing it. A few days later, we hauled the useless piece of metal back down the stairs, back into the skiff, back across to BJs parking lot, and loaded it back into our truck. We drove it back to downtown Coxen Hole.

True to his word, the man gave us our money back. We did not learn our lesson. We drove to another used appliance/furniture store, just down the main drag in Coxen Hole. It was déjà vu.

Of course, it worked, the man promised. If not, he would refund out money. Once again, we made the trip home, hauled it into the skiff, over the waterway, and up the stairs. John dragged the tools back out.

Two days later we were on or way back to Coxen Hole with the once-again useless machine in our truck. I'm sure the neighbors watching the goings-on in Oak Ridge were getting a kick out of this. You can be sure they were watching. Nothing goes unnoticed out on this little stretch of water.

Believe it or not, the second used appliance owner went in search of his keys, opened his safe, and handed us back our money. We headed straight for the newer Molineros store, on the highway. It's not really a highway, but a slow-moving, busy, two-lane road. People here call it the highway.

There, we proceeded to buy a brand-new computerized washing machine.

July 5, 2014

"Are you making any progress with the property purchase over there?" Kim asked me, as we sat on the little bench outside the front door of BJs Backyard. It was Friday afternoon, and the regular crowd was out to enjoy music by The Banditos.

She did the island point, gesturing with her chin, to the other side of the channel, where Diamond Lil is still docked.

"I need to wear a sign around my neck that says – Please don't ask about the property!" I laughed.

It has become embarrassing, after having our offer to buy accepted almost two years ago. We have spent two years waiting for the owner to get his paperwork together. We have had a certified cheque, dated August of 2012, waiting for the good news to come through.

"We are getting tired of waiting," I told Kim.

"We are beginning to think we should look elsewhere. It is such a great deal, but we can't wait forever. We cannot get a permit to build a dock. We can't even put in RECO. We have been connected to Miss Jessie's electrical box for two years now. We have considered a few other properties, but our criteria make it a challenge. We need deep water for our boat and preferably a dock. We also need enough property for Morena to graze on, with access to nice riding trails. It is difficult to find both these requirements in one property."

"I know of a couple of properties for sale up in Port Royal," said Kim. She and Joe have a house in Port Royal, to the east of Oak Ridge.

"It's totally off the grid," she warned.

"There are no services – no electricity, no town water, no garbage pickup. You would be on your own up there. There is one property for sale down by Lost Isles, she said. There is another one, further up in Port Royal, across from Fort Morgan Cay. It's been for sale for years. I bet you could get it at a really good price."

I relayed this information to John.

"I am not sure about the first property," he said.

"The second one she mentioned has been on MLS forever. It started out $360,000, way above our price range. I did notice, recently, that the price has been dropped to $180,000.

July 6, 2014

Apparently, it is a buyer's market on the island right now, so this morning we hopped in our skiff and went for a boat ride to Port Royal. The first property Kim told us about was tucked in behind some mangroves, hot, still, and buggy. We didn't stick around long.

We fell in love with the second property immediately. There was a 90-foot-long dock already in place, deep water, and 2.33 acres of beautiful land, much of it perfect for a horse to graze on.

The property had 141 feet of clean, sandy beach and an artesian well with a cistern. There were schools of large fish swimming through crystal-clear water. It was perfect for us. It seemed too good to be true.

"Could we do it?" we asked ourselves.

We had successfully lived on a boat for ten years. Much of that was spent anchored in remote spots in foreign lands. Surely, since we have lived like this for ten years, we could begin a new life, off the grid. How hard could it be?

Aug 13, 2014

"We have exciting news," I said to our group of friends at Marble Hill Farms' Crows Nest Restaurant. We had just arrived for the regular Wednesday event and, as usual, were greeted by hugs and kisses from our many friends.

"We just had our offer accepted on a beautiful property in Port Royal. Our closing date is September 30th. We are thrilled and can't wait. You are all invited to come and help us move, especially those of you who own a boat!"

It looks like Diamond Lil is about to do Port Royal!

Larry Coon aka Tie-Dye Guy (right), joining the Banditos at BJs.

The palapa at BJs backyard, as seen from the water

Rocky, after Heather bandaged and splinted his leg.

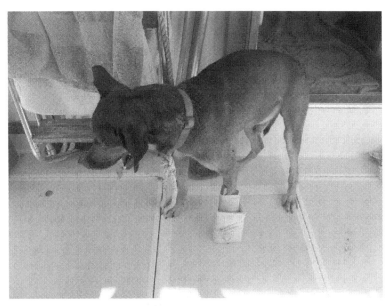

My first ever selfie taken in front of my new washing machine

Our new fridge, in our skiff, with *Diamond Lil* in the background

The empty spot in our galley where the new refrigerator will go

Debbie and John, enjoying a signature rum punch at La Sirena

The gorgeous piece of property that we found in Port Royal.

Made in the USA
Columbia, SC
13 November 2021

48917144R00161